READING THE TEA LEAVES

REFLECTIONS ON KNOWING, FLOWING, AND IDENTITY

NIECIE JONES, PHD, LMFT

DECLARATION OF LINEAGE

I am the product of the influence of many Black women. Many of my ideas and beliefs about the world come from conversations with and the works of Black women. Some of the women I am related to, most I am not.

My biological lineage includes my mom, Dianne McAdams-Jones, my sister, LaShawn Williams, and my grandmothers Amer Lee McAdams and Eunice Jones.

I am influenced by the works of Alice Walker, Toni Morrisson, and Zora Neale Hurston, whose writings taught me about Black girl- and womanhood.

bell hooks, Brittney Cooper, and Kimberlé Crenshaw provided insight into more of the academic and intellectual aspects of identity in all its different forms—race, gender, and sexuality being some of the most important ones.

Beyoncé Knowles-Carter, Solange Knowles, Nina Simone, and Corinne Bailey Rae for showing me the versatility of Black women making music.

Nikole Hannah-Jones and J Wortham for showing me what exceptional journalism looks like.

Michelle Obama and Stacey Abrams for showing me ways to work within the current institutions.

Mariame Kaba, adrienne maree brown, Angela Davis, and Alicia Garza for showing me ways to find liberation without relying on the current institutions.

Queen Afua, Tricia Hersey, and rev. angel Kyodo Williams for showing me ways to nourish my spirit amidst all the complexities of navigating the world as a Black woman.

I am influenced by queer Black women, loud Black women, "know-it-all" Black women, and I love them for it.

INTRODUCTION

I started working on this book the same way many people begin with writing books. I sensed a book inside of me that needed to be written and put out into the world. This feeling has lingered for many years, and I started working on a fiction project during my PhD program. Then, several years later, in late 2023, I received mental images of myself writing this book in the house that would later become my home. Those images came at a time when I was trying to figure out where my life was headed in general.

2023 was a successful year in my career, yet a trying year in my personal life because of expected and unexpected losses I had to grapple with. In the latter half of the year, new dreams and visions emerged that helped me to feel more myself—like I could continue to grow, develop, create, and lean into life and what it was trying to offer me. I hope the words that follow in this book can help you and others find whatever "spark" you need to keep going. Sometimes, you just need a little help or encouragement.

You may be wondering, "Who is this girl, and what can she tell me about knowing and flowing?" My parents named me Eunicia Diana Leigh Jones. Eunicia to honor my paternal grandmother, Eunice. Diana to honor my mother, Dianne. Leigh to honor Vivian Leigh from *Gone with the Wind* fame (my father's idea). I go by Niecie to pretty much everyone, and that is my preference.

I have a PhD in Medical Family Therapy, so technically, I am also Dr. Jones. Some people call me that to "put some respect on my name," but I have issues with the capitalist, elitist aspects of being a "doctor," so I prefer to be Niecie first, alphabet soup of credentials second. But if you call me Dr. Jones, I probably won't correct you. That title is also a part of my identity.

Much of my life has been spent in search of knowledge and understanding, like many of us. I was a thoughtful child, curious. Academics came easy to me, and I earned my best grades in subjects like English, Reading, and Social Studies. A lot of my time was spent reading books. One of my core memories from middle school is spending time in the library before school, during lunch, and after school. The school was shaped like a circle, and the library was right in the center of the school. Very appropriate if you had asked me, a little Black nerd who had just moved from North Carolina to Pennsylvania and found solace within libraries. I was often the only kid in there, browsing the shelves and inhaling the smell of yellowed book pages. It was familiar and felt kind. I'm pretty sure the librarians loved having me in there so often to admire the collection of books.

My dad deserves some of the credit for my love of knowledge, too. He had bookshelves of books at home, many of them about philosophy or religion. He was often in his bed or in a recliner reading a book when I went to look for him. Dad regularly "quizzed" my brother, James, and me on interesting facts. The Black history ones are the ones I remember the most. I can't remember how many of the answers I got right, but dad certainly loved to give us the correct answers with detailed explanations.

When I lived at home, my dad watched Jeopardy every weeknight, with little exceptions. He got a crazy amount of the questions (or, because it's Jeopardy, answers?) right, and we told him more than a few times to just audition for the show already so the family could get rich. Despite the number of times Jeopardy auditions were held where we lived, he never went.

I won intellectual prizes of my own, eventually. In sixth grade, I won my school spelling bee. While at Brigham Young University (BYU), I got an academic scholarship for my undergraduate studies, which helped my parents save money because they had committed to help me pay for school.

While there is definitely this academic, "intellectual" part of me, I am also a deeply emotional and creative person. I wrote poems, short stories, and songs in childhood. Often, they were about love, family relationships, friendships, and life struggles. I loved listening to music, many times choreographing dances to songs in my head. That is still something I do to this day. I have learned different art forms over the years—things like jewelry-making and painting—as a way to feel a sense of mastery, internal validation, and enjoyment. Becoming more skilled in new art forms is fun for me. Art has helped me think differently about other parts of my daily life. More on that later, though.

As a kid, I was a social creature and often the peacemaker among those around me. I liked watching people connect and facilitating connections however I could. If you had told me I would grow up to be a therapist, however, I would not have believed you. I thought I was going to be a singer, actor, or a journalist. But my formal education led me to psychotherapy, and I'm grateful for that.

Going through my therapy training and practicing for the last several years has given me opportunity after opportunity to evaluate how I understand and communicate ideas and how others do the same. It's deepened my practice of self-reflection and self-correction. As a therapist, I have a responsibility to do this work to help my clients effectively and not harm them.

I grew up in a religious household, like many people. My mother, Dianne, is a convert to The Church of Jesus Christ of Latter-day Saints, now known as The Church of Jesus Christ (and still colloquially known as the Mormon Church). My father, James, was raised Baptist. Overall, we identified as a Mormon household. Mom was the one primarily taking us to the LDS Church, and Dad took us to Baptist churches from time to time—usually on holidays like Easter or Christmas.

We also moved around a lot being in a military family, and going to the LDS Church was a constant for us because "everywhere you go, you know the lesson is going to be the same," as folks would say when I was growing up. I also noticed that something else seemed to be the same no matter what congregation I was in—my family was usually one of the only Black families, if not THE only Black family, in the predominantly white congregation. I don't think I really acknowledged this fully until I was perhaps six- or seven-years-old, as I was developing my own ideas around race and what that meant.

But there did eventually come a time when I was aware of the paradox of being Black and Mormon. I thought this was normal for a long time, since I did see other races and ethnicities in my various congregations over the years. I saw a handful of Black people at church, which seemed like enough for me, especially when I was living in North Carolina and saw Black people frequently in other spaces.

When I was 15 and living in Pennsylvania, my older sister, LaShawn, told me about something called the "priest-hood ban." She explained she had been on the internet and found out that Black people were not allowed to receive priesthood ordinances—essential rituals, rites, and authorities for salvation—in the LDS church until 1978. I didn't believe it at first. I didn't believe God or His prophets would ban any of His children from going to heaven. LaShawn insisted that this was true, though. I did what many church leaders had told me to do with difficult information throughout the years— "put it on the shelf," which means to set it aside in your mind until you feel ready to continue pondering the topic again.

It would be several years before I would take the topic off the shelf and dust it off. I still had a hard time with it because it still did not make logical sense to me. Honestly, it didn't resonate with me either in my spirit. By that time, I had read enough books and had enough experiences that gave me a Black-informed education parallel to the White-centric one I had been getting at school and at church.

I started asking more questions. How could God not be a respecter of persons also a God who banned priesthood blessings from Black people for over a hundred years? That question turned into how could that same God not see the validity and love found in gay marriages? How were God and Jesus Christ white when there is a lot of evidence that he was melanated? Why would God have Europeans "discover" the Americas and build the United States on the backs of the forced expulsion and labor of Brown and Black folks? The cognitive dissonance became too much for me to take other theological aspects as seriously as I had been taught to all my life.

My Relationship to Knowing

I eventually concluded that most knowing is subjective, shaped by our histories, experiences, biases, and neurobiology. Cultural norms determine what is "common sense" and may not be so universal as we think. Sharing ideas helps some ideas become more universally known than other, equally valid, ideas. My upbringing in a United States context as a Black female in largely predominantly white (religious) spaces created a belief system about this life and my purpose in it that helped me for a long time but eventually did not seem to help many others sharing my same experience and certainly not many others who had different experiences than mine. What I felt to be true or right shifted, and I became more open to new ideas. I became open to the truth that many things can be true at once.

When I was younger, I leaned on authority figures for guidance. I needed to learn and understand basic things in order to develop in a variety of ways—socially, cognitively, emotionally, physically, and spiritually. I eventually developed my own understanding of the world based on my own experiences and what seemed to be consistent over time. As my mental abilities sharpened, I could understand and use logic also as a way to predict or explain different phenomena. I learned to trust my intuitive experiences over time, especially for obtaining spiritual knowledge. And all the while, from the time I was a newborn, I was reading other people's responses to me and communicating my feelings as a way of social knowing. This book is partially about these different ways of knowing and recognizing their influence in everyday life. It's about knowing and being able to flow in this knowing.

Meaning-making

The journey of making meaning of my life has taken twists and turns over the years. When authority was primarily how I learned, I clung to the belief that there was a God in Heaven and that my purpose in life was to repent of my sins and return to Heaven to live with him eternally. The way I was to do that was through dependence on His Son, Jesus Christ, and living a Christlike life. So, this mortal life was a test. A test of my willingness to endure hardships and continually choose to follow Jesus and His teachings.

My intuition did tell me that there was truth to this blueprint laid out for me. Many personal experiences affirmed I was being cared for by metaphysical forces. There was a lot of success found in focusing on my education and religion, versus focusing on things that could have easily become vices for me at an early age, such as sex, recreational drugs, and alcohol. I often think I probably would have become addicted to those things.

Eventually, the ways I viewed God and Jesus Christ changed. Honestly, I was slowly shifting away from Christianity all together because the white, patriarchal lean was slowly losing its grip on my psyche. When people ask me when I "left" the LDS Church, I don't really have one particular event to point to. It was gradual, and I am still LDS-adjacent enough that language around "leaving" doesn't feel completely accurate.

I no longer practice that faith or any other religious

faith. They don't resonate with me anymore, and I don't get the intuitive hits in those spaces the way I used to. I also don't subscribe to any particular human authority figure that claims to speak for a deity or metaphysical force. At this point, there are Ancestors and other metaphysical spiritual guides that I seek out for personal guidance. Some of them belong to religious traditions, but I do not follow those traditions in any formal structure. That practice creates resonance for me as it decentralizes authority in a way that helps me tap into my personal and ancestral power. This is a large component of how I make meaning in my life now.

I would say I seek harmony among different ways of knowing, and that blend of ways of knowing has looked different in each season of my life. It will continue to shift and evolve as I develop. In my quest for knowledge, I am always balancing different truths and how they may apply in a variety of circumstances. There are often contradictions, paradoxes, and ironies. I'm comfortable being in that messy space; so much of the experience of life is messy. But I think this helps me not get caught up in my own theories of what is "right" as much as I probably could otherwise.

Knowing and flowing are key components to making meaning of life. They help us decide what our purpose is, our "why." That purpose may involve religion; it may not. Less concerned with tenets and rules of how to live, it is about the aspects of life that put the literal and metaphorical breath into our lungs. What we know shapes our beliefs about why our life matters in the grand scheme of things, and flowing can help us feel a sense of progression towards a greater meaning. It can help us truly feel alive, like we are living out our purpose.

The Importance of Identity

As we embark on this knowing and flowing journey, I want you to be thinking about identity. Social locations comprise the various identities we hold and how they intersect to locate us, among others. They shape how we know and flow. As I'm writing this, it is 2024 and a presidential election year. After the rise of diversity, equity, and inclusion initiatives following the racial reckoning of 2020, there has been push-back against these same initiatives by folks who question their effectiveness. Some have argued that these initiatives shut down productive discourse and create an intolerance of difference. I have yet to see sound research or hear stories that justify these arguments; my personal and professional experiences have shown me continually that DEI initiatives invite more conversation, awareness, and action around identity and its impact on individuals and societies.

A useful framework I have used to identify several core social locations is the ADDRESSING framework[1]. ADDRESSING is an acronym that references age, disability, religion/spirituality, ethnicity, race, socioeconomic status, sexual orientation, indigenous heritage, national origin, and gender. According to this framework, I have the following social locations within the context of the United States, where I was born, raised, and currently live: 35 (millennial), no known developmental or acquired disabilities, spiritual but not religious, mostly African and European ethnic ancestry, Black, middle class, straight, no known indigenous heritage, United States citizen, and woman.

Within these social locations, I have several identities

---

1. Hays, P. A. (2008). *Addressing Cultural Complexities in Practice: Assessment, Diagnosis, and Therapy*. American Psychological Association.

that are privileged—being able-bodied, middle class, straight, and being a US citizen, for example. I would also add that I have lighter skin as a Black person, which sometimes affords me white privilege, and that I am cisgender, which affords me straight female privilege. I also have oppressed identities, being Black and female. I also have been considered fat at different points in my life, which has affected my social experiences quite a bit.

Acknowledging where these privileges and oppressions exist allows me to have self-awareness as I interact with others. It also invites me to consider how others are experiencing me. It helps me consider the social locations of others and where power may be present in our interactions. There are spaces where I am ignorant because of the experiences I do not have and don't have intimate knowledge of. So, I invite you as the reader to remember my social locations as you consider my perspective. And I invite you to consider how yours shape how you know and flow.

The Book's Title

"Reading the tea leaves" is a reference to knowing and understanding your circumstances. It is an idiom, with origins in divination, that refers to predicting the future. In some spiritual traditions, someone drinks a cup of tea and then takes part in a reading of tea leaves left at the bottom of the cup. There may be meaning in the size, shape, and type of individual and collective tea leaves. The reader uses their knowledge of the tea leaves and their own intuition to determine what information the querent needs to know regarding their circumstances.

My mom used this phrase during my interview with her. She used it to refer to what some of us may call "reading the room," usually socially, to understand how she would interact or behave based on what she observed. My mom's historical context includes references to the occult, such as hoodoo, in addition to the accepted spiritual tradition of Christianity. References to tea leaves, rootwork, goofer dust, and conjuring are not uncommon to hear in the southeast United States, where she and my dad are from. While my family did not actively talk about any of these "demonic" spiritual traditions when I was growing up, there have been some integrations culturally through language and other practices that have persisted. It is no coincidence that they are related to how my family has come to know things and how that has been passed down, especially when it comes to how we move around in society. Some of our knowing and flowing is just in our DNA.

The Structure of this Book

This book is divided into three parts. In part one, we're going to go over some of the basic ways of knowing. It is not exhaustive by any means because folks have conceptualized so many ways of knowing. To keep it simple, I will talk about five different ways of knowing: authority, reason, experience, intuition, and social cognition. These ways of knowing may seem new for some of you and a review for others. Take what is relevant to you, and don't worry about the rest. This part will lay the foundation for how we come to understand things as "true" or "right." I'll talk about how each of these ways of knowing can be helpful and harmful to demonstrate the subjective nature of knowledge. I will then provide you with some experiments in knowing, which will allow you to test out how you come to know things.

Part two is about flowing. This section will focus on how

we get into an optimal state of awareness and attention. We'll get into the conditions of a flow state and how we can create them. We'll also talk about what can block flow and how to break through those barriers. There will also be experiments in flowing to help you find your own flow.

In part three, you will get a practical application of knowing and flowing via my family. Over the years, people have expressed interest in the individual and collective wisdom of my family. Through interviews with family members from several generations—the silent generation, Boomers, Gen X, Millennials, Gen Z, and Gen Alpha—you will see unique patterns of how my family knows and flows. You will see how there is variance in how my relatives do things and what factors might account for the sameness and difference.

PART ONE

A "candid" photo of me during my master's program

1

WHAT IS KNOWING?

My first semester of my graduate studies was in Fall 2014. I took classes at Utah State University at the bottom of Old Main Hill, where the Marriage and Family Therapy program was housed. The students I would take classes with were people I liked, and I was excited to start the journey of becoming a therapist. I was also nervous to have smaller class sizes where I would be expected to speak up more and share my ideas. I was more of a perfectionist back then. I was worried about getting concepts wrong or having unpopular opinions. I feared others wouldn't think I was worth listening to, as often happened in other spaces.

One of my classes that year was family theory. My professor, Dr. Bradford, taught us about a branch of philosophy that I had never heard of before — epistemology. This branch is about the theory of knowledge. It's about how we know things. This was the first time that I had considered more objectively the different ways of knowing, specifically four that were taught in the class: authority, reason, experience, and intuition.

The importance of these four ways of knowing is because of their ability to lead to theory formation. Theory, one of academia's favorite tools, is any group of ideas intended to describe or explain, usually. Theory is especially important in fields like psychology and sociology, where research uses theory to produce evidence that supports or refutes it. It helps to determine whether sound logic and evidence are informed by research and practice.

Theory and the ways of knowing that inform it are a big deal for folks who are working in professions like mine, as psychotherapy should help people improve their quality of life. If a theory can be proven to be true under certain circumstances over time, that information will likely be helpful for others. Therapists are trained to use evidence-based interventions to improve interpersonal relationships in and out of the therapy room. Evidence-based interventions come from research. Research is based on theory.

At the same time, therapists use not only evidence and logic to help clients. This became clear as I started seeing clients during my master's program. We use our intuition often to determine what clients need. We can pay attention to the energy or vibe in the session and notice when it shifts. Sometimes, we get a sense that there is more going on with clients than what our experience has taught us. By following this sense, we can make important breakthroughs during the client's therapy journey.

The Ways of Knowing: An Introduction

So, what are these four ways of knowing that I mentioned earlier? Authority refers to an entity that is trusted to be a source of knowledge, usually because of specific credentials or expertise. You trust their words over your own understanding, perhaps because you lack expertise in their domain. Growing up, I believed God was my Heavenly Father, Jesus Christ was His Son, and that there was a living prophet on earth that communed with both of them to receive revelation for the entire world. I believed these things to be true because adults at church and my mom told me they were true. They were the only beliefs related to spirituality that I knew for a long time. I did not know that I could think otherwise, as I was in the early stages of my cognitive development.

Reason is about logical ideas following each other consistently. It typically relies on other ideas already accepted to be true. When I was younger, I was taught that if the Book of Mormon is true, then Joseph Smith was a true prophet of God, and the LDS Church is also true. The reason presented to me was entirely predicated on the veracity of the Book of Mormon. That was the true statement that led to the other conclusions about Joseph Smith and the LDS Church. I assumed this was all reasonable until I understood more about how logic has its faults.

When there is an observation via the physical senses of an event, this is considered to be experience or evidence. When I went to the LDS church anywhere I moved growing up, my family was often one of the only Black families in the predominantly white congregation, or we were the only one. From seeing this happen over and over, I reached the conclusion that in the LDS Church, there were not a lot of Black people but a whole lot of White people.

Intuition involves knowing through physical and metaphysical senses, having no other way of knowing to support it. It is having a general feeling about something. I often had calming and euphoric feelings when things resonated with me at church, especially as I got older. I would have some thoughts or feelings that simply felt like they were right. They weren't always pleasant thoughts; sometimes, they were unpleasant and accompanied by a sense of calm.

There is a fifth way of knowing, however, that I did not learn about in graduate school. At least, not explicitly. Social cognition is a type of knowing that is distinctly interpersonal and involves understanding others' perspectives. It is about seeing others as unique individuals and that our experiences will not always be the same as others. When I was a young adult in high school and college, I began to better understand the feelings of queer folks inside and outside of the LDS church. This affected my personal ethics moving forward.

These ways of knowing are influenced by our histories, our prior knowing, and the biases we carry. I was raised LDS as a Black female. Because my family was in the military, I moved around a lot as a kid and interacted with different people. I assumed the world only had absolute rights and wrongs in my childhood, as determined by my family, my religion, and my limited lived experience. As I matured, I learned that knowledge is not that simple or binary.

Curious Questions

1. How did you learn "knowing?"
2. What ways of knowing do you use?
3. What experiences have you had with the 5 ways of knowing presented in this chapter?
4. Which way(s) of knowing do you tend to rely on the most?

Presenting research at a conference

AUTHORITY

M y earliest memories include going to the LDS Church every Sunday with my family. Once, as a small child, I was in a stroller next to my family's pew and given water in a small sacrament cup. My mom was later scolded for hydrating her child with the symbol of the Lord's blood.

When I was a little older, I attended Primary, which was the programming for young children 3-11 years old. We learned songs from the LDS Children's Songbook, many of which still hold special memories for me. We sang songs about Heavenly Father and Jesus Christ, early Mormon pioneers, and loving thy neighbor. One of my favorite songs was "I Feel My Savior's Love." This song represented a lot of my feelings about seeing the Divine in everyday life, in the people I was around, in nature, in music. I felt like I could feel Jesus's love when I wanted to access it. It helped me feel safe and hopeful, even when things weren't going well.

Most importantly, however, in Primary we learned songs about following the prophet of the church.

Follow the prophet, follow the prophet,
Follow the prophet; don't go astray.
Follow the prophet, follow the prophet,
Follow the prophet; he knows the way.[1]

Even though the song was written in a major key, it had an ominous tone—a warning to those listening. I was being taught who I needed to trust in order to be seen as good and righteous in the eyes of God. This song talked about several Biblical prophets and then admonished me to follow the modern-day prophet because we were living in "a world where people are confused."

Every six months in the LDS Church, there is a general conference for the worldwide church where the current prophet and his right-hand men (and sometimes women)—called general authorities—give talks. They tell church members where to focus their attention to be prepared for the Second Coming of Jesus Christ. The conference lasts for 8-12 hours on a weekend, and members are encouraged to attend as many sessions as they can. When I was older and attending a church class called seminary every morning before going to my high school classes, I could make up for missed days by watching general conference and taking lots of notes.

The messages I took from the general conference talks spanned many topics considered to be eternal essentials. I was told why marriage between a man and a woman was sacred. I was taught that leaving the church and forsaking my covenants was sinful and hypocritical to others that I had brought into "the fold." One general authority preached

1.   Hiatt, D.E. (1989). Follow the Prophet [Song]. *Children's Songbook.* Intellectual Reserve, Inc.

about how it is a choice to be offended, and we can also choose not to be offended.

There were some talks I really loved and others that made me raise my eyebrows. The eyebrow-raising increased in frequency over the years as my other ways of knowing kicked in more intensely. I had more experiences that showed me that some of what I was being taught wasn't exactly true universally, if at all. My intuition let me know some messages were "off" and not representative of how the Divine really felt about the earth, its inhabitants, and the metaphysical realm. Some messages did not make logical sense to me. My social cognition kicked in when I recognized the harmful impact some messages were having on people I loved and cared about.

Authority: The Concept

We lean on authority to receive guidance where we feel there is not enough. We call people experts when they have a lot of knowledge or credentials in a certain area. Parents and caregivers are authorities. Spiritual leaders are authorities. Teachers and medical professionals are authorities. Government officials and celebrities are authorities. To become such experts, it is generally expected that these authorities have been validated in some way over time for their consistency and accuracy with their expertise. That validation can come from licensing boards, the academy, or adoring fans.

How Authority Helps Us

Authority can be helpful for us as a starting point when learning new information. When I was younger and needed an example of how to live my life, being in a structured environment with rules and expectations did help me. My family and my childhood faith shaped my worldview in ways that taught me to value kindness, family, and education. I was not yet in a place to shoulder the responsibility of knowing topics so deeply. My cognitive abilities needed time to develop. While I was not yet able to discern things as well as I can now, having authorities to guide me supported my cognitive development. I learned new information as I got older and could process it more effectively.

How Authority Harms Us

Authorities can be misleading with the information they claim is true. Some of the things I learned from LDS prophets and other church leaders were disparaging towards BIPOC (Black, Indigenous, and People of Color). That conflicted with my lived experience as a Black person. I was taught that Black people were not worthy of receiving temple and priesthood ordinances for over 100 years. Church leaders taught me the founding of the United States was ordained by God. I learned that the Lamanite people written about in the Book of Mormon—the most important book in the LDS faith—were the dark-skinned ancestors of Native Americans. Consequently, the Nephite people of the same period were described as light-skinned, and sometimes people went as far as to say they were white. This was meant to be a juxtaposition between good and evil, and it justified early Mormon pioneer racism towards indigenous Americans.[2]

Authorities may become experts based on popularity

---

2. Much of what I've mentioned in this section was taught to me in church

and fame rather than more rigorous forms of validating their expertise. Celebrities can often become seen as experts on topics they do not have intimate knowledge of because their adoring fans want to trust them and be like them. Additionally, authority can harm us by hindering our own critical thinking skills when we rely on them too much. Without personal critical thinking skills, identifying our own preferences, morals, and ethics can become difficult. This becomes more important as we mature and become adults who are expected to live independently to a greater degree than when we were children.

Authority can silence our curiosity. Curiosity is a practical tool for understanding ourselves and the world. It encourages us to question what we think we know and helps us see things in a new light. It drives us to explore and learn more, which is essential for personal growth and adapting our knowledge.

The Impact of Colonization on Knowing

We need to acknowledge the ways entities considered authorities have dominated ways of knowing for centuries. This has been to the detriment of humanity as a whole because they have consistently discarded the voices of minoritized and marginalized people. White, western, male ways of knowing have been considered "right" and "true" in places affected by colonization and arguably most of the rest of the world. The LDS church has taken part in religious and territorial expansion using practices that have ranged

---

as interpretations of scripture verses from the Book of Mormon and the Bible. Some of these teachings can be found online and in archives.

from indigenous cultural erasure to physical violence.[3] This is in keeping with the global history of colonization via religion.

To exert their dominance and "rightness," European colonizers found reasons to dismiss the wisdom of indigenous people around the world. This was based on primarily physical features, such as skin tone, body size and shape, eye color, and hair color/type. They even created a branch of science called eugenics to justify this treatment.[4] Eugenics has now been discredited by modern scientists, though there are still groups of people who hold on to these antiquated ideas.

Interestingly, colonizers have found ways to pick and choose which elements of indigenous wisdom to pass off as their own and which elements to discard and bastardize. Many elements in the Yoruba religion, which is older than Christianity and may be one of the oldest religions in the world, are also found in modern-day Christianity. The idea of a Supreme God in Christianity can be traced back to Yoruba's Olódùmare. The Holy Spirit in Christianity can be described as one's Orí, or Higher Self, in the Yoruba religion. Rituals such as singing, dancing, and praying to deities were practiced by those in the Yoruba faith long before Christianity used similar practices. The belief in an afterlife and what happens in that space also existed for devotees of the Yoruba faith for centuries before Christianity existed.[5]

---

3. See literature on the Mormon Meadow Massacre and Mormon treatment of enslaved Africans.

4. National Human Genome Research Institute. *Eugenics and scientific racism.* https:// www.genome.gov/about-genomics/fact-sheets/Eugenics-and-Scientific-Racism

5. Fasola, A. F. F. (2014). *The holy Odu: A collection of verses from the 256 Odu Ifa with commentary.* Fategbe Fatunmbi Fasola.

However, modern-day Christianity regularly bastardizes African Traditional Religions because to accept and honor it would violate the commandment of not worshipping any gods other than the Christian god.[6]

Another way colonizers have simultaneously co-opted and dismissed indigenous wisdom has been through the use and abuse of plant medicine. Many plants used in spiritual ceremonies by indigenous people have been criminalized because of their psychotropic properties and the harmful side effects of using such plants in certain ways. Examples include cannabis, ayahuasca, and peyote. Some plants may be used under special circumstances, such as when administered by a licensed medical practitioner or shaman, but are illegal to possess in most, if not all, other ways.[7]

On the other hand, colonizers have co-opted the use of many plants for medicinal purposes by mixing them with other chemicals, giving them scientific names, and then selling them for much more than is affordable or accessible to folks who really need the medicine.[8] Ketamine, a man-made medicine that comes from a fungus that is found in nature, is a medicine used often for those with treatment-resistant depression. Several therapy clients of mine have spoken of the life-altering effects of ketamine on their depression and traumatic stress.

I would be missing a giant opportunity if I did not call

---

6. See Exodus 20:2-4 in most versions of the Bible.

7. United States Drug Enforcement Administration. *Drug scheduling.* U.S. Department of Justice. https://www.dea.gov/drug-information/drug- scheduling#:~:text=Schedule%20I%20drugs%2C%20substances%2C%20or,)%2C%20methaqualone%2C%20and%20peyote.

8. Megli, D. (2024, January 30). The ketamine economy: New mental health clinics are a 'Wild West' with few rules. National Public Radio. https://www.npr.org/sections/ health-shots/2024/01/30/1227630630/ketamine-infusion-clinic-mental-health- depression-anxiety-fda-off-label

out academia and its colonizer ways. The formal education system, an institution of colonization, often teaches us that those with doctoral degrees and specific training possess the most correct knowledge. Having the time, money, and resources to obtain anything beyond a bachelor's degree is difficult for many groups who have been historically disadvantaged. Costs of education and the dark hole that is student loan debt are huge deterrents for those seeking more education and skills. Yet, scholars are the ones who create "best practices" for fields such as education, law, medicine, and psychology. Western philosophy created and used the scientific method,[9] which we will discuss more in the "Experience" chapter.

They conduct research studies and write up reports of the results. The biases present within the research are ignored by the common consumer, and the generalizability of the results is hardly considered. I cannot tell you how many studies I've read that had homogenous research groups and no meaningful conversation around folks who might not fall into those groups. I've also participated in research that had questionable methodology and was dismissed when I brought up concerns about how the methods could skew the results.

Western science decided that quantitative methodology was the most reliable type of data and that randomized controlled trials were the golden standard of research. Did you know the average randomized controlled trial can cost between $43 to over $100,000 per participant?[10] How many

9. Hepburn, B. & Anderson, H. (2021, June 1). Scientific method. Stanford Encyclopedia of Philosophy. https://plato.stanford.edu/entries/scientific-method/   #:~:text=Aristotle%20is%20recognized%20as%20giving,methods%20of%20inquiry%2 0into%20nature.

10. Speich, B., von Niederhausern, B., Schur, N., Hemkens, L. G., Fürst, T.

marginalized groups have access to that kind of money to do research on the things that matter to them that might legitimize their experience in substantial ways? I can't think of many, if any.

While these white, western, cisgender, heterosexual male ways of knowing have tried to create more objective and absolute ways of understanding, there are many other ways of knowing that are resurfacing and reclaiming their rightful place as paths towards wisdom. Alternate understandings of historical events are becoming more popularized, creating concerns for those who have traditionally been used for supremacy and dominance. Many folks—specifically women of color—are leading the charge to decolonize history, therapy, gender, and racial hierarchies.

My Current Relationship with Authority

Currently, I would say I look to authorities for their expertise on new topics. I look at the source of where new information comes from and if I deem it to be trustworthy. I pay attention to what news outlets report and tend to consider more moderate or left-leaning outlets to be more trustworthy as authorities. That being said, I don't solidify everything I hear as knowledge right away. I will consider what's being said and compare it to other things I've learned.

As someone who loves to read, I also find certain authors to be authorities. I read primarily nonfiction—lots of sociology and psychology books. I love Black feminist

Bhatnager, N., Alturki, R., Agarwal, A., Kasenda, B., Pauli-Magnus, C., Schwenkglenks, M., Briel, M., Making Randomized Trials Affordable (MARTA) Group. (2018). Systematic review on costs and resource use of randomized clinical trials shows a lack of transparent and comprehensive data. *Journal of Clinical Epidemiology, 96,* 1-11.doi: 10.1016/ j.jclinepi.2017.12.018

literature and consider many authors in that genre to be my teachers. Their work resonates with me and my experiences. They teach me more about life as a Black woman and how that may affect my experiences. They have prepared me for much I have come up against.

Just because I consider some entities authorities does not mean they dictate my actions or behaviors. I admit there is influence there, but I am pretty open to other perspectives. I believe knowledge is mostly subjective and not whittled down to only certain things being true. I like to experiment with different truths and stay curious.

Curious Questions

1. What authorities have you looked to for truth in your life?
2. What have you learned to be true from authorities?
3. What makes people authorities to you in this season of your life?
4. How much do you rely on authorities for knowledge?

~

At the Missionary Training Center

3

REASON

I n 2010, I got to fulfill one of my dreams by serving an LDS mission for 18 months. I was so excited to serve the Lord and bring converted souls to Him. I spent months preparing, filling out applications, going to medical appointments, reading all the mission literature I could get my hands on. I started my mission service by spending 9 weeks in the missionary training center (MTC) in Provo, Utah. I was smiling so hard the first day I got there that my cheeks hurt. I believed I was entering a new chapter of Mormon womanhood. It felt like there were two points of entry at 21 years old—marriage or mission—and I chose mission. I was assigned to go to Brazil to start my mission service after my time at the MTC.

There were a few core texts you used when serving a foreign mission: the scriptures, Preach My Gospel (PMG), the missionary handbook, and some language materials that would help you learn the language faster. Preach My Gospel (PMG), which is still used, is a guide of sorts for missionary work. It contains the missionary lessons that you teach to potential converts, called "investigators," as well as the invitations you extend to them after the lessons. I had an English version of PMG, a Portuguese version of PMG, and I even had a mini English version of PMG that I purchased and read before my mission had even started. These core texts were utilized daily to help me become a better missionary.

Missionaries also had a variety of classes and talks we attended. Their purpose was to better prepare us for "the real world" of the mission field. One talk was by a young man around my age that I think had served a mission and was then imparting his wisdom to the rest of us. He was addressing some common concerns that people have prior to joining the LDS Church. Race and the priesthood was one of those topics. He said the best way to handle that, and any other concern, was to redirect people to the Book of Mormon because once folks had a testimony of the Book of Mormon, that should quiet any other concerns. Basically, don't get caught up in the race stuff.

When I left the MTC, I ended up serving in Alabama for several months until I could get my Brazil visa. As you can probably imagine, the race stuff came up. Almost daily. And my white missionary companions often asked me to help them "explain" this to their Black investigators. I was open to doing this, even though it felt uncomfortable at times. There was one Black male investigator I remember well when it came to this topic. He was being taught by another set of sister missionaries and attended church in the same building as my companion and me. He was visibly excited about what he was learning and liked the people at church.

Then, his friends and family "got" him by telling him about the temple and priesthood ban. He was discouraged and disappointed that the missionaries had not told them about that themselves. The missionaries, both white, panicked and asked me to talk to him. I met with him and talked to him about his concerns. I think I validated him and then told him that at the end of the day he was a child of God and God wouldn't permanently ban any of His worthy Children from being with him. I may have even said something like, "None of that matters anymore. What matters is you are able to have the priesthood now." This answer makes me cringe now, but it was what I could come up with at the time. I did not like going the "trust your testimony of the Book of Mormon" route because I did not think that reasoning was sound when joining the church was such a big decision. I think he heard me because he looked less anxious at the end of the conversation. However, he ultimately decided against joining the church.

Once I was in Brazil, there was a different culture around missionary service. There seemed to be more urgency, and it felt like missionaries were expected to approach the work more like salespeople. Instead of being prayerful about which invitations to extend to investigators, we were encouraged to invite people to be baptized as members of the LDS church if they received spiritual confirmation that the Book of Mormon was a true book from God. And we were encouraged to do that while teaching them for the first time.

I was not convinced this was a great idea the first time I learned of this method. It felt like too much to ask of others. But eventually I was persuaded that this was not too much pressure. After all, they didn't have to get baptized if they didn't receive that spiritual confirmation. As I reflect on that approach now, I recognize that the logic was not as sound as I thought back then. I was asking people to base membership in a religion on having one special emotional experience. I understand that for some people, their intuition may have told them to join the church because that was the right move for them (more on that in the "Intuition" chapter), but for many others, I think there was not a logical balance to justify joining the church. I was just telling them that if they knew the Book of Mormon to be true, then being baptized a member of the LDS church was the logical next step.

That leads into other types of mission logic I was taught, especially while I was in Brazil. My leaders repeated much of the same logic they had learned from their leaders. If you work hard enough, then people will get baptized and remain active members of the church. If you pray hard enough. If you talk to enough people. If you teach enough lessons. Basically, if I was productive enough and produced the right "numbers," the Lord would bless me and the mission with baptisms because I'd earned them.

This was drilled into me, but if I'm being completely honest, I never fully believed it. When I tried to live by that kind of logic, my companions and I often experienced anxiety around doing enough to be seen as valuable and worthy in our mission. The spiritual piece that led me to serving a mission felt silenced in favor of getting the right numbers to make leadership happy. My diligence as a missionary was often questioned by my younger male leaders, who were not always truthful about their numbers. The logic did not add up, and neither did the numbers.

Reason: The Concept

Reason is a way of knowing that follows other rules of logic. It seeks consistency with other ideas. It is a "common sense" way of knowing as we learn more and more ideas and how they are expected to fit together. There are a few types of reason worth mentioning that can help explain how people use their logic: (1) inductive reasoning, (2) deductive reasoning, and (3) abductive reasoning.

Inductive reasoning starts with specific information and then generates a theory of what may be true on a general level. On my mission, I encouraged investigators to use this method:

1. They usually already had a belief in God and Jesus Christ.
2. I helped them develop good feelings about the Book of Mormon to influence their decision to be baptized as LDS Church members.
3. Then, because the LDS Church also includes a belief in God, Jesus Christ, and the Book of Mormon, some of those investigators then made the general conclusion that the LDS Church was the right church for them to join.
4. As they continued to gather more information, their reasoning would become more solidified over time.

Deductive reasoning works in the opposite direction. It starts with general information and then works to make more specific conclusions. I used logic like this on my mission, as well. Baptism was often a tense topic that came up because there is the belief that it is not enough to be "saved," like many churches talk about. You must repent of your sins, be baptized by the "proper authority," and then receive the Holy Ghost by a priesthood holder. Some investigators struggled with the idea that they had to be rebaptized when they already went through that ritual and were committed to God. The logic I shared with them, as taught in PMG, went something like this:

1. All baptisms must be ordained by God.
2. The LDS Church is the only church with the appropriate authority from God to baptize others.
3. Therefore, the LDS Church has the only type of baptism that is ordained of God.

A third type of reasoning is less talked about but important for us—abductive reasoning. Using evidence given, you make an educated guess in the case of a lot of uncertainty. Unfortunately, this type of reasoning was used to try to explain why God would permit a temple and priesthood ban for Black people for over a hundred years. I heard many "educated" guesses over the years. The initial flow of logic usually went like this:

1. God has a reason why He does what He does.
2. God speaks through prophets.
3. The prophet instituted a temple and priesthood ban.
4. God instituted a temple and priesthood ban.

Possible reasons to further support this reasoning via best guessing included:

1. Black people were not worthy of receiving temple and priesthood blessings.
2. Black people were not ready to receive temple and priesthood blessings.
3. Black people were not meant to receive temple and priesthood blessings, as they were meant to be eternal servants.

4. Black people did not need to receive temple and priesthood blessings.

This was pretty confusing, as there did not seem to be room for another possible conclusion: God didn't institute a temple and priesthood ban.

How Reason Helps Us

There is comfort in feeling like things are common sense. Common sense, meaning that many other people would come to the same conclusions. It is logic that is generally accepted as true. Some common sense reasoning for someone who grew up in a religious household might include things like:

1. There is a God.
2. God loves you.
3. God wants you to be a good person and do good things.

We carry many of these common sense ideas with us all the time. They help us navigate situations and make decisions quickly, based on the information we have.

How Reason Harms Us

When we look at reason more closely, we see that reason deals with abstract ideas that may not apply in the real world. In other words, the reasoning may not be practical when you try it out. You may receive evidence that disproves the logic.

Logical fallacies are arguments that can be disproven by

other reasoning. There are several types of logical fallacies,[1] and I will mention a few common ones to get you thinking. The "straw man" fallacy is one where someone oversimplifies an argument in order to make it easier to attack. This is symbolized as setting up a straw man; he's not real or created with any substance. The original argument is then not fully addressed, but a similar or even entirely different argument is being addressed instead. This can create the illusion of debunking the original argument.

I see this logical fallacy used often to justify bigotry. An important point of discussion in the LDS Church regards the legitimacy of gay marriage and the place of LGBTQ+ folks as a whole. Where LGBTQ+ advocates have outlined several times in a variety of ways the legitimacy of queer relationships, LDS Church leaders have repeatedly simplified the argument to marriage being between a man and a woman and gender (meaning sex assigned at birth) being an eternal principle. This response ignores the original point of whether queer relationships can also be legitimate.

There are also false dilemmas that folks create. The false dilemma fallacy simplifies a complex issue in terms of two polarized sides. It is misleading because it claims that there can only be two outcomes to consider, rather than acknowledging that most issues can have a spectrum of outcomes.

Using the mission logic I was taught, I presented investigators with two outcomes of their actions—they were either following Jesus Christ by being baptized the Mormon way, or they would not be able to live eternally with their families, God, and Jesus Christ. It was presented as an all-or-nothing choice, which I'm sure created anxiety for people

---

1. See a list of common logical fallacies here: https://blog.hubspot.com/ marketing/ common-logical-fallacies

trying to make decisions about joining the church. In Mormon theology, there are different "glories of heaven," which are essentially different levels of heaven. I suppose those might be points on the spectrum of outcomes, but the way I presented this to folks made it sound like other points on the spectrum were basically like being in hell. It was a way of manipulating people into believing there was only one correct way to make an eternal connection with your family possible.

Correlation does not equal causation. Anyone who has taken a statistics course has probably heard this phrase. More people should take statistics because the phrase is true. Correlation refers to two events or conditions that are present at the same time. Causation means that one event or condition is causing the other event or condition. Many times, researchers will present data and explicitly state whether events are correlated or if there is substantial evidence that one event caused the other. Unfortunately, by the time this information gets to the lay reader, what may have originally been reported as correlated now is being reported as causation.

Using the reasoning introduced earlier in the chapter, we can see how correlation can be assumed to be causation. The LDS Church had a policy to bar members of African descent from temple and priesthood ordinances. The reasoning used to justify this policy often correlated lack of access to ordinances with unequal standing[2] between Black and non-Black church members. Many people went further to assume this unequal standing caused the lack of access to temple and priesthood ordinances. This, therefore, elimi-

---

2. This is code used by white people to excuse their racism.

nated the need to look further into reasons this ban could have occurred and remained in place for so long.[3]

It can be difficult to understand or accept ideas that make little sense to us. Sometimes, because we can't understand, we decide that those ideas can't be true. This is how the personal incredulity fallacies works. Just because we don't understand something, that does not make it automatically false. We are humans who have a variety of ways we learn and process material. Some of us have higher processing speeds, while others process information more slowly. Some of our prior knowledge is based on limited understanding of other concepts and ideas, and when we hear ideas that contradict with what we believe to be true, it may take several more points of contact with the idea before we accept its veracity.

This fallacy comes into play any time a person who has been treated poorly tries to explain their experience to someone who has a more privileged lived experience. Without prior experience with the situation, it can be difficult to accept someone else's reality—especially if it doesn't make logical sense to the privileged person. This is the case at times with sexual assault and domestic violence. Folks who know the perpetrator and/or do not understand the patterns of abuse may have a hard time believing the perpetrator did what the victim alleges. Often, these folks having a hard time believing the victim are in dominant positions and may be removed from such events or choose to be dismissive. This fallacy can lead to great harm when not checked.

In addition to logical fallacies, we should also acknowledge that common sense thinking is more rooted in socio-

---

3. The reason was racism.

cultural norms than reason in many instances. Normal customs, such as greetings, vary from culture and culture. Additionally, norms around social structures like romantic relationships and expressions of spirituality can look vastly different from region to region. Therefore, reason can be a hindrance if we are trying to apply the same common sense thinking from one culture to another.

My Current Relationship with Reason

I use reason daily, mostly to manage scheduling and regular tasks. I am definitely a "Type A" person; organization, to-do lists, and systems that run well are things I love. Reason is one way I get curious about new things I've learned via authority. It helps me decide how legitimate I think an authority's expertise is. Reason is also intertwined with experience because I will use reasoning more once I have an experience in order to process what happened.

Using reason isn't a preferred way of communicating for me, though I inevitably use it in my personal and professional lives. In high school, I participated in mock trial and debate team, but in this season of my life I rarely make reason a big part of conversation with others both on and offline. I find that I get exhausted of trying to reason with people when I feel like we came into the conversation not really willing to look at other ways of thinking and are not making any progress in better understanding each other solely through logical arguments. I didn't enjoy doing that on my mission, and I still don't enjoy it now.

I don't think reason is as powerful in expanding perspectives as experience and social cognition. I find reason to be a helpful building block in conversations, but it can only get us so far. Also, my experiences in academia working with colleagues and studying scholars have shown me continually that there is a gap in the theoretical and the practical. Folks who spend more time theorizing without lived experience of the theory's application are often removed from reality to some extent, and I decided early in my career that I did not want to fall into that trap.

Curious Questions

1. Where is the logic sound in Niecie's shared personal experiences?
2. What logical fallacies have you been taught to be true?
3. How do you use logic as a knowledge source?
4. When has reason turned out not to be true?

At a debate tournament in high school

4

EXPERIENCE

I spent my early childhood in places with more BIPOC children around me, and I felt like I was well-liked and belonged. I noticed that my body started to mature earlier than my friends, and this brought both welcome and unwelcome attention. My friends and I giggled about our crushes and then squealed when we learned someone liked us back. I was excited when it was my turn for the cutest boy in class to show interest in me.

And then I moved to Pennsylvania in the Fall of 1999. While there were some BIPOC kids at school, there were significantly less and then virtually none at church. I was the new kid, which was not a new thing for me, but it was the start of middle school, when social relationships became more important to my daily life. I started noticing how differently people were treated and saw cliques. My family lived in an area with wealthier families and, therefore, more resources for the schools my siblings and I attended. The popular kids were typically thin, wealthy, and white. The rest of us had to stand out by either being attractive or funny.

Sixth grade holds a lot of core memories for me, and it may be one of the most pivotal years of my grade school life. This was the time when I started noticing my peers dating each other. I was in on the conversations my friends were having about dating, but I was always a listening ear, an observer. I don't recall ever being the object of anyone's affections, though I had plenty of crushes that were not reciprocated. Some of them were loudly not reciprocated, which was embarrassing.

Still, I remained an integral part of the social scene but was excluded from the more "coupled" activities. Once, at the dentist, the dental hygienist working with me—who was one of my schoolmates' mother—asked me if I had a boyfriend, and I said no. Then she proceeded to tell me that she was so glad her daughter didn't have a boyfriend this year because then she wouldn't have to spend money on a Valentine's Day gift. I had never received a gift from a romantic interest, so I don't remember saying anything in response. Also, I was at the dentist, so I was probably not sure what to say with a mouth agape. That experience was a reminder of the ways I was excluded as I was entering my teen years.

High school was not much better. I moved to Utah in 10th grade, and this was my introduction to a new breed of white people. While New England white people were wealthy and Catholic, Utah white people were middle class and Mormon. One of my earliest Utah memories was driving down a road in Lehi and watching someone casually riding a horse down the same road. It ended up being a girl I went to school with, whose family owned a ranch. Ranches were popular in Lehi and the surrounding areas, like Eagle Mountain. At school, there were mostly white kids, followed by Latine and Polynesian kids, and then a handful of Black,

Asian, and Native kids. I looked up the racial demographics of the school once, and Black people were virtually non-existent percentage-wise.

I was able to find some good friends, and we got through Lehi High School together. We talked about dating, as well, and it was a little different in a predominantly Mormon area. Teens weren't encouraged to date until they were 16, and, even then, not to really do it exclusively until they were older and intending to marry. I saw my friends going on dates, and I went on a few when there were dances. There were several school dances every year, and some required boys to ask girls while others had girls ask boys. Gender non-conformity was not a consideration here. Also, if you didn't have a date but wanted to go to the dance, you could go "stag," which meant going solo or with friends. I went to many dances stag.

Other than dances, I can only recall a few dates I had while in high school. My best friend, who was white, was going on a date with a boy she was getting to know, and he wanted a date for his best friend. So, my friend asked me if I would go on a double date, and I said yes. I had never been on a blind date before. Had I been on *any* dates before? We went to the movies, where we were supposed to meet up with the boys. My bestie and her date were friendly with each other right away. My date, on the other hand, looked disgusted to see me. He was cold towards me the entire night and did not talk to me beyond one or two words here and there. He left as soon as the movie was over, while my friend, her date, and I stuck around to chat.

I commented on how rude my date was to me, and his friend gestured to me and said something along the lines of, "Well, he wasn't expecting *you*." I knew what he meant. He wasn't expecting a Black girl. In fact, I knew that the moment his friend started being rude to me. My best friend had a hard time accepting that this could be the reason why he behaved so strangely.[1] I felt like I had to keep explaining my experience to her, and eventually she seemed to understand. That boys would not be excited to date a Black girl was a new concept for her. For me, this was just more evidence to support my theory around the Black girl dating experience in predominantly white spaces.

Middle school and high school showed me time after time that Black girls were not seen as true dating material for white people and even some BIPOC. I continually had the experience of watching most, if not all, of my other friends going on dates and having reciprocated romantic interests, while I didn't for the most part. The only exception of someone I dated with a reciprocated interest was my Latino boyfriend, who I dated long distance for a few months during senior year. We met at a college preparation summer camp for multicultural (non-white) high school students held at Brigham Young University. Even then, he and his parents did not want us to be exclusive too soon, and I always wondered if I was more into him than he was into me.[2]

After learning of more Black teen girl experiences, I realized that Black girls not dating a lot in predominantly White spaces was more of the rule than the exception. This seemed to be true, inclusive of our skin tone, religious affiliation, body type, and size. Of course, those factors play a part in who may have been "preferred" to date among us, but collectively we were experiencing more or less the same

---

1. This is a good example of the personal incredulity fallacy I mentioned in the Reason chapter.

2. Spoiler alert: I was more into him. He later came out as gay.

thing. These experiences led to my conclusion that race played a significant factor in my dating life, and that knowledge informed how I approached dating later in life. It also informs how I approach therapy with my Black female clients, who are experiencing much of the same thing.

Experience: The Concept

Experience, also known scientifically as empiricism, is about looking at and experiencing observable events as facts. We gain more experiences that support or challenge different theories we carry with us. We are constantly being shaped by the experiences we are having. Experience is the foundation of the Western scientific method. There are variations of the basic method that have been developed over time. The basic idea is that using this method creates more objectivity—a kind of psychological distance between the observer and the observed. If it is more objective, there is a higher likelihood that the same phenomenon can be observed by others and confirmed as true. If many people can see the same thing as true, this decreases the likelihood that it will be seen as untrue or false under the same circumstances.

How Experience Helps Us

Experience is helpful in everyday life. It provides sensory evidence that is hard to be refuted. In my adolescence, it was observable by myself and many others that my peers were going on more dates than I was. Experience can help establish patterns of events that help us rely on a theory being consistent over time. In Pennsylvania, I had the same issue with both white LDS and non-LDS men when it came to dating. I don't think I dated any BIPOC men, either, in middle school. That led to a theory about dating that helped me understand similar patterns in high school. Living in Utah County as a teen yielded little dating opportunities for me with white LDS men, who were most my dating options at the time.

How Experience Harms Us

Like other ways of knowing, experience has its downsides. We can rely on experience to the point that we create generalizations, which do not account for all experiences in all situations. I know of some Black women who dated several white men as teens and adults. Some Black women feel white men are more open to dating them than Black men based on their experiences.

We also need to make room for neurodivergence, which is more than a cluster of disorders, but a way to acknowledge how differently people process information. Neurodivergent folks can have more heightened sensory experiences compared with neurotypical folks. This can significantly change how events are experienced. Our senses can also be manipulated, whether we are neurodiverse or neurotypical. Optical illusions are wonderful examples of how things do not always appear as they seem.

So many ideas and concepts we accept as being real are not observable. Therefore, they cannot be experienced universally. We cannot observe love or time objectively, but there are cultural connotations around these ideas that deeply affect how they are experienced.

My Current Relationship with Experience

Experience has probably been the biggest source of knowledge for me as an adult. My own lived experiences and the shared experiences of others have shaped a lot of my current worldview. Experience has debunked several entities I once considered authorities and has proven to be a more reliable source of knowledge.

I lean on experience a lot when making decisions. I am able to remember pleasant and unpleasant experiences from the past as I consider options for the future. Experience can highlight fears I have based on things that have happened in the past in areas I am not as confident about. It can help me move forward when I'm anxious about something because I have the memory of instances when I did the same thing before and was successful. Experience has taught me what environments help me flow.

Curious Questions

1. How do you see the scientific method playing out in the story Niecie shared at the beginning of the chapter?
2. What personal experiences do you have with knowing through experience?
3. What helps you to trust your experiences?
4. How has experience harmed you?

Doing a card reading session

5

INTUITION

My freshman year of college brought a lot of changes for me. I'd moved out of my parents' house to live on-campus at BYU less than 30 minutes away. After breaking up with my high school boyfriend, I was newly single. We were both at BYU and spent time together pretty often. My roommate was one of my best friends from high school, and that provided the typical challenges of adjusting to how different people live. I got a job on-campus cleaning offices and classrooms to get out of my apartment, make some money and also give my mind a break from thinking about how much I missed my ex.

One night, I was overwhelmed by what felt like the many losses I was going through—my ex, one of my best friends, and probably any chance at love in the future. I was at work, and I think I had finished up all of my duties for the night. In solitude on my supervisor's couch, I said the most heartfelt prayer I had until that point. I asked God to tell me what to do to address these things in my life that were making me so sad. After the prayer, I sat and listened for answers, like I had been taught to do growing up.

What followed was the clearest montage of images that gave me guidance about what to do. I saw images of me talking to my roommate to clear the air, but now, over 15 years after that event, I can't remember the rest of the images I saw. That experience changed the trajectory of my life, still, because of what I learned about my ability to "see" answers, solutions, and even the future at times. I realized that I'd had similar, less intense, experiences over the years. Usually, they were in my dreams and not images that could come when I was conscious. But when I had that experience at work that night, I knew I was onto something and that it was big.

After that, I started to pay more attention to the images that came into my mind's eye, both invited and uninvited. I dreamt that my ex started dating someone else, and then I found out not long after that this had actually happened. A couple of years later, I had fantasies about a missionary I had an interest in while on my LDS mission, and one of them came true exactly as I had envisioned it. In my fantasy, we would be at a church fireside, I would be in the choir, he would see me on the big screen, and then come find me to talk to me afterwards. I prayed that God would make this happen. I did all the things I needed to on my end. There was a choir to join for an upcoming fireside, and I joined, knowing that my face would likely be shown on TV while I was singing. The night of the fireside I trusted I would be on the big screen, and then I waited. I heard the young man's voice behind me—a voice I had not heard in over two years—and turned to see him there, looking at me with a smile on his face. We did end up talking and connecting on social media after that.

While I was at BYU, I had a couple more fantasy-to-reality experiences with him. I was hopeful that we would be together long term because the experiences I was having were in line with LDS ideas of following "promptings" of the Holy Spirit. Sadly, while I had several dreams and fantasies about us getting married, that did not happen. I decided to hold on to what I learned from the experience, even if I had to let go of the idea of the two of us being together.

Over the years, I have honed this skill of clairvoyance, which is the metaphysical knowing of something via images. I have been able to visualize many things I've wanted and brought those things into my life. You could argue that these are things the Divine already wants for me and, when I'm aligned, I visualize them as if they were my own thoughts. I don't think that is necessarily untrue, but I don't truly know what the source of my visions is or spend too much time thinking about that. Some of them have played out exactly as I've imagined them, like the previous example I gave, and some of them have happened but differently than I imagined.

I started learning how to read tarot cards in 2020. I studied different card decks and interpretations of the cards from several readers. The pictures on the cards, along with my intuition, created a spiritual blend that excited my senses. In July 2021, I was drawn to a tarot card called "the magician." I decided I wanted to embody that energy that month. Part of that included creating the love life I wanted. I was already receiving a lot of signs that the right energy was present to make this happen. I was on dating apps, with some luck, but not finding quite the right person I wanted to date long-term. When I read my tarot cards, I often got the message that the kind of person I'd want to date was around if I continued to be patient.

I had recently gotten into candle magic and lit a 7-day candle to bring in the kind of man I could marry. While it was burning, I was journaling about this man and how I envisioned him. I did a meditation to visualize the kind of person he might be. I saw two men in those meditations. The first was a light-skinned Black man who had locs. He was sitting in the lotus position with his eyes closed. The second was a dark-skinned Black man on a plot of land he owned and worked on. He was looking at me with a big smile on his face.

Within a week of lighting the first candle, I met the first man after matching on a dating app. Oddly enough, I didn't really realize he was the man from my meditation until after we'd met in person. He was light-skinned and had locs, but he also had glasses. He wasn't a yogi or anything close to it, but he had a chill vibe about him. We dated for a year and a half, and we talked about marriage. I knew early on that he was someone I saw myself married to. He knew he was going to move out of the country, however, so while there was definite potential, it was not fully realized in that relationship.

Intuition: The Concept

Use of the physical and metaphysical senses to understand or know something without other reason or evidence to support it is known as intuition. A lot of folks call it a gut feeling or a certain vibe they get. Most, if not all, people experience "intuitive hits," or moments where they receive an intuitive sense about something via physical feelings, hearing, seeing, or knowing. Sometimes, smell, touch, and other bodily senses are part of these intuitive hits, but in this book, we'll focus on what are known as "the four clairs"—clairvoyance, clairsentience, clairaudience, and claircognizance.

The Four "Clairs"

Clairvoyance involves knowing through the sense of sight. Sight includes physically seeing something or having mental images. When I spoke of my clairvoyant experiences earlier in the chapter, I was referring to the mental images. Using the tarot cards to receive intuitive hits could be considered a type of clairvoyance, as well, though I am using my physical sight to draw conclusions that others may or may not make based on the images on the cards.

You may be clairsentient if you understand and know things through feelings. This could be a physical feeling, such as goosebumps, a queasy stomach, or aches in your shoulder. You may have pleasant internal feelings about something and call it a good vibe. I tend to refer to this as energy and notice if I sense pleasant or unpleasant energy from a person or situation. When I met both of the men I mentioned earlier, I immediately got good vibes from them. Those persisted for a long time.

Knowing through the sense of sound is called clairaudience. These can be external sounds that you hear or sounds you hear in your head. I often hear sections of songs in my head that I have not heard for years. Often, their lyrics would have something to do with a current situation or something that was about to happen.

Claircognizance refers to knowing through thoughts. These can be thoughts that don't seem to originate from you but feel like they are applicable in a situation. I've had thoughts pop up in my head to take a different route to a destination, and at times I've avoided harm or seen something pleasant, like an old friend. With the missionary I mentioned at the beginning of the chapter, I eventually started having the thought, "He's never going to be brave enough to marry you." It was uncomfortable, but I knew it was true.

How Intuition Helps Us

Intuition adds a lot of depth to our lives. It is our own personal, direct way of knowing. With intuition, we develop the understanding of something without the direct influence of other people. It can also give us confirmation that something is true or real. Intuitive hits can be deeply emotional and life-changing for us as well. The experience I shared from my freshman year earlier in the chapter laid the foundations for many more clairvoyant experiences that I had after. Intuition helps us to trust ourselves and our instincts. It shows us that we are not wholly dependent on others for knowledge and can access understanding for ourselves. My clairvoyant experiences have helped me trust myself and how I have lived my life up to this point. They have helped me develop my sense of self.

How Intuition Harms Us

Like other forms of knowledge, intuition has its limits. We can mistake our own subjective knowing for objective knowledge. This is common in many spiritual groups, and some extreme groups that we call cults. Oftentimes, one person will have a self-described spiritual, or intuitive, experience that gives them information about something, like a forthcoming apocalypse. They may have dreams about this apocalypse or get a physical sense of when it will come. But many folks have had these feelings and the ending of the world as we know it has not yet happened. I've also had dreams about the end of the world, but I have been careful with how I share those dreams and the meaning I've ascribed to them.

It is hard to validate someone's intuition. There haven't been consistent methods for proving someone's instincts, especially in the Western world. Our "hunches" about things are not always shared by other people, and they are not easy to explain. Additionally, our mental health can impact our senses. Folks who experience auditory and visual hallucinations may be receiving sensory messages in or out of sync with cultural norms and values. Some people have the instinct to kill others, and this may or may not fit with cultural expectations. Such instincts are labeled as severe mental health disorders, such as schizophrenia.

My Current Relationship with Intuition

I try to stay in tune with my intuition as often as I can. My first impressions of a situation are usually guided by my intuition. Sometimes I am off with my assessment, but most of the time I am reading the environment correctly.

I do card readings for myself to start off each week. I've been doing that for over 3 years now. Since 2020 I've kept a card reading journal to keep track of my readings and how different topics develop over time. I'd say about 85% of what I've read for myself has been accurate about my life. This rate is pretty similar to how accurate I believe others are when they read for me.

I pay attention to the mental images that come to me in

dreams and waking life. Sometimes they mean something significant, and other times they are meant to pass by without much thought. I kept a dream journal for 3 years and recently stopped to give myself a mental break. I will probably pick up the practice again in the future.

I have also been listening to my body as an intuitive practice for a few years now. I pay attention to when it wants movement, food, water, and sleep, among other things. I started eating intuitively to improve my relationship with my body. This has led to a journey of better understanding the impact of dieting on my body. I have changed my work schedule to match how my body best can best work, given the impacts of capitalism upon it.

Curious Questions

1. What types of intuition do you possess?
2. How do you let your intuition guide you?
3. When has your intuition been off?

~

Speaking at one of the first vigils I helped organize

6

SOCIAL COGNITION

Many people described me as a diplomatic child. Friendships were easy for me. I tried to make sure people felt included. By the time I was in elementary school, I spent time around many types of people and was exposed to many cultures. I could understand what different kids needed, what made them feel good, and what made them feel bad. Reading my friends and their parents was a skill I used mostly for good but sometimes for ill.

Adults and children often saw me as a leader, and I liked creating special interest groups with my friends. We got together to create dance numbers, sing karaoke, and have sleepovers on Halloween night. As I got older, had more experiences, and went to college, I still had the diplomatic quality, but I was not as social as I had been in childhood. My time was spent more on my academic life and preserving my Black girlhood rather than socializing and not feeling understood by my white peers. I had experienced some social burns in that area and had internalized those experiences. As I was developing cognitively, I was also developing racially, which created both moments of clarity and confusion as to how I fit in the world.

By the time I was getting ready to go to graduate school, I had formed more ideas about how I had been socialized. I realized I had spent many years assimilating to white people's expectations and felt more of a desire to explore what existed outside of that mindset. I became more aligned with Black feminism, Black liberation, and other philosophies that centered Blackness.

When the killings of Black people in the US started gaining more media attention and public outcry in the early to mid 2010s, I—like everyone else—was watching. I watched traditional media. I watched social media. I watched how my non-Black friends were responding versus my Black friends. It dawned on me that the white people I thought would have had my back if I were in trouble probably wouldn't be concerned with me if I were a random Black person unjustly handled and harmed by law enforcement. This didn't sit right with me, and I distanced myself from many of these people that I used to consider friends.

Black pain became a focus in a way it had not been before. I noticed what triggered it. I saw how people reacted differently to the pain. Instead of condemning acts of violence in response to state violence, I recognized the need to take time to understand the hurt. I reflected on my own pain and how I was handling it. I felt a desire, like many, to do something. It was a tall order, and still is, to know what to do in times of great crisis because often the crisis is a symptom of a much larger problem that people posting their outrage on social media or attending protests couldn't solve. For me, those were accessible ways to do something, but they did not seem like ways I could address my pain and use my skills in a beneficial way.

When I spoke with my community about things that might be helpful, I realized that creating space to mourn and organize was important. So, while some found it helpful to attend rallies and protests, I and some others organized vigils. We had moments of silence, space for folks to share their feelings, and words of encouragement to help with the days and weeks ahead. When I was organizing these spaces, I felt more connected and purposeful. I met many people who would become good friends in similar situations in the future. I highlighted the talents of people I knew and allowed them to channel their feelings in ways that aligned with them. This was the best way I could show my community that I could see them and show up for them.

Social Cognition: The Concept

From the time we are babies, we are practicing social cognition. This is the knowing that we gain by being in contact with other people. It is a uniquely interpersonal knowing, whereas perhaps the other ways of knowing don't directly involve other people. Social cognition requires it.[1] As infants, we learn how to distinguish the facial features of a known caretaker from a stranger's. We use it to understand what it means when facial muscles move—to recognize emotions such as happiness, sadness, surprise, and disgust.[2]

Our brains consist of mirror neurons, which become activated when we perform an action or when we see

---

1. Amodio, D. M., & Frith, C. D. (2006). *Meeting of minds: the medial frontal cortex and social cognition. Nature Reviews Neuroscience, 7*(4), 268–277. doi:10.1038/ nrn1884

2. Haxby, J. V., Hoffman, E. A., & Gobbini, M. I. (2000). *The distributed human neural system for face perception. Trends in Cognitive Sciences, 4*(6), 223–233. doi:10.1016/ s1364-6613(00)01482-0

someone else performing that same action. This suggests that we can mirror others' actions and emotions, which is understood to be empathy. Folks who identify as having high levels of empathy likely have mirror neurons in their brains that are often activated by others' actions, triggering a sense of understanding and connection.[3] Empathy also involves the capacity to take on others' perspectives, emotions, and motivations. If you can engage in perspective-taking, you are likely better able to handle complex social situations and build meaningful relationships.

A lot of my early understanding of body language and social norms was from a white, Western, Christian male context. While I could read others from this context, others —using this context—would view me as angry or disinterested because I wasn't smiling as much as women and girls were expected to. I used to get confused by this, but over time I stopped caring so much what others using viewing me from this context thought of me. There were things I recognized socially based on my experiences that ended up serving me well in a variety of other social situations.

How Social Cognition Helps Us

Social cognition benefits us daily. We need it to successfully work with others. It helps us form and maintain social connections. Whether we are working on relationships with our family of origin or family of choice, social cognition helps us create attachments and do things that will benefit the family. It is part of our instinct to survive. While I did

---

3. Decety, J. & Claus, L. (2007). *The role of the right temporoparietal junction in social interaction: How low-level computational processes contribute to meta-cognition. The Neuroscientist: 12*(580). doi: 10.1177/1073858407304654

not grow up having a general distrust of white people, that grew over time. I learned that tuning into Blackness and Black people in my life, there was a safety I found and am still cultivating. It feels like developing a Black social cognition has helped me to, in fact, survive and thrive in a white supremacist society.

How Social Cognition Harms Us

As you can probably tell, social cognition can also be a detriment. Unfortunately, it can be used to manipulate other people's emotions. We see social cognition used for ill in affinity groups where there is a common identity that unites its members. There are plenty of get-rich-quick schemes founded by folks from marginalized positions that use that position to gain loyalty from others, though the ulterior motive is to make the founders rich rather than improve the position of those sharing their common identity. While there are plenty of these same schemes founded by white cisgender heterosexual Christian men—such as the many multi-level marketing companies found in the US —the social and financial impact can be more devastating for the marginalized groups who are targeted.

Additionally, social cues can vary depending on culture and context. Direct eye contact, for example, can be interpreted as a demonstration of active listening in one context —such as in the US. In another context—perhaps in some places in the Global East—it may be seen as disrespectful or an assertion of dominance over another person. Physical touch has varying levels of significance to people, depending on prior experience, brain makeup, and other factors. Not everyone can pick up on social cues that would be typical of their cultural context. We have research on how folks can detect trustworthy and untrustworthy facial patterns, and those with differences in brain function may see these facial patterns differently.

My Current Relationship with Social Cognition

Social cognition is required for the work I do as a therapist, consultant, and general healer. To determine how I will respond, I tap into what others are saying and doing. I enjoy using social cognition to have deeper connections with others and to help them connect with themselves. My goal is to be diplomatic and understanding with others.

This "knowing" I have about people has helped me navigate different relationships over the years. It's fairly easy for me to read body language. My understanding of other cultures—especially Black culture as I was growing up—gave me an expanded perspective on how to "read" other people and how they approach interpersonal relationships. Over time, I've recognized more how I have been able to get along with neurodivergent folks pretty well due to my openness to difference and have further honed that skill through my therapist role.

Curious Questions

1. How would you describe the development of Niecie's social cognition?
2. What do you know because of social cognition?
3. How can you develop more social cognition inside and outside of your typical environment?

~

Getting my mind blown by a card reading from Ellen Bowles

7

BALANCING WAYS OF KNOWING

I 've been seeing spiritual healers since I was a child attending the LDS Church. At that time, they were in the form of spiritual leaders, usually white men. When I got older, specifically when I was in graduate school, I began seeing spiritual leaders outside of a religious context, namely intuitives and mediums. They used tarot cards, oracle cards, sound healing, energy, and even drawings to intuit the information that I needed to know. To date, only one of those sessions has been unhelpful. I've been able to find the truths–large truths that were relevant for the time I was receiving them–in most sessions, and I am grateful for those.

Yet, I also need to note that my relationship with those healers and how I felt I was understood spiritually, psychologically, and emotionally was impacted by race and how it showed up in those sessions.

My first session with an intuitive healer was with a Native American and European woman in Sedona, Arizona. It was an unplanned stop I made with some church friends, and I loved the session we had. It was under an hour and full of information that proved to be useful in that moment and in the months ahead when I started my PhD studies. She mentioned that I would be doing creative work, likely off the beaten path of what I thought a professional career was supposed to mean. She knew that I wanted to work with disenfranchised groups. She spoke to me tentatively about what could be possible but was careful about using definite or absolute language. She made sure I had her information so I could reach out if I wanted to. I've kept up with her for the last 6 years and have received several readings from her. I still trust her readings and feel an energetic bond with her.

At one point during those 6 years, I lost touch with her because she left the organization she did readings with. So, I started receiving readings from whoever was in store the day I needed a reading. Those were, to my knowledge, all done by white women. They were good readings–again, most of my readings have been helpful–but they were not like my first intuitive healer. The white women who did my readings sometimes focused on how I was "too masculine," a trope that has a long, racialized history when it comes to white supremacy and femininity. They didn't seem to have a background of or sensitivity to how their spiritual lens may have been white-centered and anti-Black.

I reached out to a mixed Black female tarot reader in May 2021 for a birthday reading. It was the first time a Black person had done a session for me. It was an hour long, and she immediately picked up on the Haitian spiritual connection I had been feeling for several months, though I have no Haitian ancestry that I know of. She talked openly and freely about Voodoo, Hoodoo, and Ifa. This made sense because both sides of my family are from South Carolina and have spoken of some of these traditions as parts of their upbringing: African deities and methods of reaching them.

She gave suggestions and advice on how to move forward. She mentioned that I might visit New Orleans in the next year, which was something I had been wanting to do and something I did end up doing in April 2022. I kept the video recording of that reading and the notes I took and referenced them often.

While in New Orleans, I sought out another Black intuitive healer for a session. I was not able to schedule the one I wanted, but I did have one with one of the in-store readers at her shop, who happened to be another Black person. They were genderfluid from what I could tell, and we had a great session. They didn't mention anything about race in their reading, but the cultural references in the store and in our exchanges helped me feel understood and honored for my spiritual journey. They told me some things I didn't understand/agree with, but they were gentle in their delivery and how they suggested I go about understanding the situation being presented. They did what I prefer readers do–tell me what they're seeing from a tentative and not definite lens, sometimes abstractly, and invite me to do the deeper work of spiritual connecting, understanding, and healing over the next several weeks and months. I did that work and referenced the notes from that reading often. I also did what I normally do after an intuitive healing session—focus on what resonates with me the most and leave the rest alone until I feel called to revisit it. And sometimes I never feel called to revisit it.

Several months later, I was in Northern California for work. After a work session, I went to a metaphysical shop and requested a reading with an in-store reader. This was done by a white woman who also was a therapist before turning more of her energy to spiritual work. She gave a great reading and hit on many of the topics I had been thinking about, as well as how I had been reading those topics in the frequent readings I did for myself. She was fairly direct and sounded more "final" in her predictions.

Her body language and verbal language let me know she didn't think reading for myself so often—or maybe even at all—was a good idea. "I don't even read for myself!" she let me know, fairly matter-of-factly. I had heard this idea from other readers (all of them white), and I decided that this was not the way for me. I knew my Ancestors and Spirit Guides were sending me messages and trusted me to interpret them for myself. Reading for myself helped me deepen my ancestral connection, find the kind of romantic partner I wanted, start my businesses, and leave my corporate job, among other things. I went to others for readings periodically to get other information, but I also could intuit when I could receive certain answers myself without others' interpretations—which was and is most of the time.

To top things off, at the end of the reading, she told me reading for myself was giving me a "slanted" perspective. As if each and every reading is not slanted due to our interpretations of intuitive messages based on our background and experience. I was turned off from that style of reading, though much of the information was helpful.

My most recent experience with a white spiritual healer ironically happened on Thanksgiving 2022. She had followed me on Instagram some weeks prior, and I ended up setting up an appointment because I thought it might be a nice cleansing experience for the colonizer's holiday. What ended up happening was a combination of several culturally appropriated practices with no acknowledgement of where the practices came from. The icing on the cake was when it came to clearing blockages. She told me one of the blockages was ancestral, which she had not experienced before. She then said she sent out the atonement of Jesus Christ to my ancestors and that they accepted it, which cleared the blockage.[1]

My initial reaction was to be curious. I admitted that many of them were Christian, so I could understand that. But I was also surprised and uncomfortable. Those feelings grew later in the day as I thought more about it. While I understand a lot of spiritual practitioners use different practices, including religious ones, there was something deeply unsettling about a white woman not asking permission of the direct descendant of an ancestor if extending a practice that is believed to "save" someone is okay during the direct descendant's own healing session. It just added to the colonizer feeling of the day, and I was pretty disappointed. She also did a small oracle reading at the end of the session, and I can't remember any of what she said to me.

Decolonizing Knowledge

Colonization has created quite a conundrum when it comes to what is acceptable as knowledge and who gets to determine that. It can be extremely difficult for some folks to feel comfortable in their skin when there are "facts" that tell them how they exist is somehow wrong or unacceptable. It can prevent folks from discovering and accepting parts of themselves that are not wrong, only unique and different. It can prevent us from accepting each other as fully human. In her book, *All the Black Girls are Activists,* author EbonyJanice writes of the concept of decolonizing authority. She says the

---

1.   I did a tarot spread about that situation later to ask my ancestors if they really accepted the atonement. The 5 of swords and 10 of swords let me know that was a pretty loud "HELL NO" from several of them.

goals of this decolonization are self-determination and sovereignty. She says, "...one would have to heal themselves from the idea of being subordinate in order to truly inherit their divine right to be even as credible and free."[2]

As we look to decolonize who gets to determine knowledge and what is knowledge, we would benefit from looking at the most marginalized identities as sources of deeper knowledge. These folks see the world at levels and with layers that those who are less burdened by oppression just will not have. They are the most qualified to comment on how systems are working, both the functioning parts and the dysfunctioning parts. If systems are working only for some people to promote wholeness, it is not working as well as it should be for everyone.

Much of the way we see ways of knowing and who can be an expert have an individualistic, binary slant, particularly in a western context. We see things as all or nothing, either and or. Those of us who display these characteristics in our private and public lives struggle many times to embrace more collective, non-binary stances when it comes to knowing. Lama Rod Owens, co-author of the book *Radical Dharma,* writes this about his queer Black male identity:

> When I realized that queerness couldn't be limited to sex and sexuality, that to choose queer expressed something more profound about who and how we are, I had to shift my worldview to one that sees beyond binary truths handed to us to yoke ourselves into a system of control. To

---

2. EbonyJanice. (2023). *All the black girls are activists: A fourth wave feminist pursuit of dreams as radical resistance.* Row House.

hold queerness as a practice is to be in active radical acceptance of everyone and all things as they are.[3]

Applying this type of queer wisdom to social causes has
proven to be beneficial to society and advancing access to
rights. More importantly, they are beneficial because they
simply exist and add richness to the lives of their communities with their worldview. We need to be listening more to
our queer siblings at the intersection of race, gender, disability, and socioeconomic status.

To further challenge the individualistic, binary ways of
knowing we are used to, we must embrace collaborative
knowing. Some call this the co-creation of knowledge. As a
therapist, some of the post-modern or less traditional
models of therapy that I embrace involve taking what is
called a "one-down" position. This is done in an effort to
remove the role of "expert" from the therapist and shift it to
the client, as clients are the true experts of their lives. They
are the only ones who can truly know their experience,
though I can gain a lot of insight about them from therapy
sessions. My role, then, becomes a witness and co-creator of
the experience they want moving forward. I stand beside
them in the quest for knowledge, staying curious during the
process. We question, challenge, and validate perspectives,
as those in dialogue do.

Along the same lines of moving away from staunch indi-
vidualism, we need to work on decolonizing credentials.
This does not mean that I think we should get rid of credentials entirely. We need to broaden how we consider someone
or a group as being "legitimate" when it comes to knowl-

---

3. Williams, A.K., Owens, L. R., & Syedullah, J. (2016). *Radical dharma: Talking race, love, and liberation.* North Atlantic Books.

edge. In academia and beyond, we need to be curious about credentialing.

In the practice of psychotherapy, there are training programs we have to go through, usually at the graduate level (master's degree or a doctoral degree). Then, we have state and/or national licensing exams we take. These courses and exams include laws and ethics that we agree to adhere to. Some of these laws and ethics promote harmful practices, such as involving state institutions when our knowledge about what heals and what harms tells us that such involvement does not always align with our values. There are criminal charges and licensure suspensions for therapists who make the decision not to involve state institutions when the state and the licensure board believe it was necessary. In these circumstances, there is often a lack of deeper conversation around what professional, cultural, and systemic knowing was involved in making a controversial ethical decision. The law and the licensure board, influenced by larger systemic and societal forces, win by default.

Psychotherapy is not the only field with ethical dilemmas, such as the one mentioned above. Many fields have them. Even the best science, often called "best practices," can be and has been proven as harmful in light of more knowledge. Science is not definite; it is always shifting and evolving to become more accurate and applicable in a variety of circumstances. Unfortunately, we often treat science as if it is infallible when this is not the case. Therefore, we need to make space for other ways of knowing outside of western science and allow for different types of expertise as valid. We need to look at how culture plays a part in different fields and how indigenous knowledge has made valuable contributions as well as local perspectives.

Grappling with Hard Truths

It would be wonderful if every time we were presented with new information, we immediately updated or reprocessed all the historical information in our brains. However, this is not the case. We have an easier time processing some new bits of information more than others. The bits we have a harder time with may conflict with the historical information we have stored. In psychology, schems are what we call the patterns of information stored in our brain. Every bit of information we receive is processed and integrated into a previously created schema or possibly creates a new one. Examples of schemes include stereotypes, archetypes, and social roles. Perhaps schemas are the basis for the biases we have.

If new information conflicts with a schema that it may seem to match with, our brains do our best to understand the new information according to the pattern the schema has already developed. Possible ways of processing the new information include distorting it (sometimes called assimilation) or changing some of the existing beliefs to accommodate the new information.[4] There are theories that the schema does not change much over time, which may explain why folks tend to hold on to some of the same ideas over the course of a lifetime, even where there is evidence to the contrary.[5] We often need to have multiple events of crit-

---

4. Smith, W. (2022). *Piaget's schema & learning Theory: 3 fascinating experiments.* PositivePsychology.com. https://positivepsychology.com/piaget-schemas/.

5. Cherry, K. (2023). *What Is a schema in psychology?* Verywell Mind. https://www.verywellmind.com/what-is-a-schema-2795873#:~:text=When%20learning%20new%20information%20that,the%20of ace%20of%20contradictory%20information.

ical engagement with new information in order to restructure our schemas.

In high school, the only boyfriend I had let me know he struggled with same-sex attraction, a phrase that was embraced widely by the LDS Church. We broke up and remained friends in college. It was a hard time for me, though, because I thought I would marry him. He was my first love. There was a part of me that was worried that I would lose the chance to be with him to a man, and I struggled to process that because I understood how to be jealous of and in competition with women, but not a man.

He left on a two-year LDS mission to South America, and we wrote to each other from time to time via email and snail mail. While he was gone, there was a big push for California's proposition 8, which would ban same-sex marriage if passed. I was attending BYU, and there was buzz all around campus about the importance of voting yes to "prop 8," even though we were in Utah and not California. I was told the implications of not getting politically involved were large, even though the LDS Church asserts a generally politically neutral stance. My professors and church leaders, considered to be the authorities on the subject, were telling me I needed to advocate for this proposition.

I initially did not like the idea of prop 8; it felt pretty invasive to tell people who they could and could not marry based on sex or gender. I really thought the LDS Church and BYU's involvement in the campaign to vote yes was unnecessary, considering there were so many more worthy social causes to put power behind. But I was trying to be an amenable Mormon, so I sat through the lectures and discussions on the topic.

Then I listened to a talk by the prophet of the church at the time, Thomas S. Monson. I remember getting an intuitive hit that he was right about keeping marriage between a man and a woman, and that changed how I viewed gay marriage. I even wrote a letter to my high school boyfriend to tell him about my experience and that I knew the prophet was right, even if it didn't totally make logical sense to me. He responded and thanked me for my testimony. Not long after he returned from his mission he came out as a gay man. Now he lives in New York City with his partner, and they seem very happy.

I'm so glad he ultimately did what was right for him and did not continue relying on church authorities or my intuition. I've fully accepted gay marriage since that time, and I've wondered over the years why I got that intuitive hit about the sanctity of traditional marriage only to later shun that idea. But then I remember that I've had plenty of intuitive hits that felt right at one point and then were disproven or became irrelevant over time once I had more information through experience or reasoning. I've become more cautious about who I share intuitive hits with and around what topics.

When I read tarot or oracle cards for others, I give a disclaimer beforehand that they should pay attention to the parts that resonate with them rather than accept everything I say as fact. I am a human vessel, colored by my own biases and experiences. I actually think my concern that my high school boyfriend would eventually marry a man likely primed me to receive an intuitive hit about the "rightness" of traditional marriage, though it was an unconscious thought. By balancing and blending my different ways of knowing, I was able to get to a place of acceptance.

Curious Questions

1. How do you see Niecie balancing ways of knowing in the personal experience she shared at the beginning of the chapter?
2. What truths have been hard for you to accept?
3. What ways of knowing have helped you decolonize knowledge?

8

EXPERIMENTS IN KNOWING

The following exercises are meant to help you become more aware of and expand how you understand things. I've used them in my own life and see the value they have added to my life. They are not comprehensive, and you may have found other ways to hone these skills. Take what you want and leave the rest.

Debate Exercise

PURPOSE

This exercise is intended to help you develop your critical thinking skills. You may notice a mix of reason, authority and experience coming into play here as you go through the steps. It is an exercise to help you recognize sound logic and logical fallacies and engage with those more meaningfully.

. . .

<u>STEPS</u>

1. Choose a debate to watch or listen to. An argument of some sort will work, too. I suggest a recent political debate, as these can bring up contrasting views that often trigger emotional reactions for us.

2. Research the background of the people involved in the debate. Pay attention to where they are viewed as authorities or experts. Note their platforms if they are political candidates.

3. Review the types of reasoning mentioned in the "Reason" chapter. Also, take a look at a list of logical fallacies and decide which ones you want to listen for.

4. Watch or listen to the debate. Make a note every time you hear an argument using sound logic. Make a note every time you hear an argument using logical fallacies. You may want to pause the debate periodically to make sure you can really break it down and make sense of the logic being used.

5. After the debate, look at the notes you made.

<u>REFLECTION</u>

1. What logic was the most compelling? Why?
2. Who used the soundest logic to you?
3. Who used more logical fallacies?
4. What information or context would have made the logical fallacies more sound?

5. What experiences have you had that support or don't support the arguments made?

6. What other arguments could you make to support or refute the arguments made during the debate?

7. What other interesting things did you notice about the debate

Card Reading Exercise

PURPOSE

For this exercise, you'll be tapping into your intuitive senses — specifically clairvoyance. Using the visual images on the cards and your own intuition, you will "read," or interpret, the cards and determine the message they are conveying.

To do this, you will need a deck of oracle or tarot cards. They are similar but different in some ways. Both types of cards usually have images and/or words on them. They can both be used to receive guidance, clarity, and understanding concerning the past, present, or future. Oracle cards can have any number of cards in the deck. There are usually under 100, so the deck is easy to shuffle. Every oracle deck has its own theme and interpretation system, usually found in an accompanying guide book. Tarot cards usually have the same 78 cards in a deck, even if the theme/imagery of the deck is different. Each card has a general meaning based on tradition, though plenty of readers deviate from the general meaning based on how their intuition leads them.

For example, a general meaning of the "hanged man" card would be feeling stuck in some sense. I could theoretically pick up any tarot deck and read the hanged man card as meaning feeling stuck. What may change the meaning of that card, however, is the cards around it if that card is part of a "spread." A card spread is a layout of cards that is meant to be interpreted. Some spreads only consist of one card, some contain 3, some contain a dozen. The number really depends on the reader and what the purpose of the spread is. Take a look at this spread I did about a trip I took.

Trip Spread
7/29/23
Date

SPREAD

Q: What else do I need to Know?

INITIAL IMPRESSIONS

There may be some stuckness I feel where I want be able to successfully logic myself out of it to defend myself. I will need emotional balance and feeling- There is a sense of looking for something I can't find, maybe w/ money or values.

LATER REFLECTIONS

8/28: The airline lost my luggage @ the end of the trip!.

AT THE TIME I did this spread, I was a few days away from going on the trip. I was getting anxious and wanted some clarity about what I could expect to happen on the trip. You can see the hanged man card in the first row was the first card I pulled. I then pulled the rest of the cards in the top column to start getting a picture of the situation. From there, I pulled "clarifying" cards, which are in the second row. Each card on the second row clarifies the card right above it in the first row. I know this will sound confusing to some people; trust me, it makes more sense as you practice card reading!

As I pulled cards, I started to get the general sense that not everything was going to go according to plan. The third row of cards — with the four of cups and three of wands reversed — is what really got my attention. The image on the four of cups looked like a flamingo searching for something it couldn't find. I also knew the three of wands often meant waiting for the fruits of labor. Since the card was reversed, the meaning turned into likely not seeing the fruits of labor. To me, this reinforced the card right above it. I had a sense that I would be looking for something that I just would not be able to find. You can see the full interpretation I made of the spread initially in the "Initial Impressions" section of my journal page. What ended up happening right at the end of my trip was that my luggage didn't make it home! And despite my best efforts to get it back, I never got it back. According to the AirTag I put inside it, it is still at the Antalya, Turkey airport to this day. I recorded my "later reflections" at the bottom right of my journal page.

STEPS

1. Choose a card reading deck.
2. Shuffle the deck with the intention of clearing the energy around you and the cards.
3. Select 1-3 cards and lay them out in a spread.
4. Look at each card and note your initial impressions.
5. Pay attention to the visuals on the cards and how they may interact with each other.
6. Read the guide book, if there is one, for further possible interpretations of the cards
7. Write down or record what resonates with you from the messages you feel you are receiving from the spread.

REFLECTION

1. How would you describe your experience with this activity?
2. What felt easy?
3. What felt difficult?

Dream Interpretation Exercise

PURPOSE

This is another exercise designed to strengthen your intuition. Dreams can embody many senses as you are experiencing them, so you can potentially develop all of your metaphysical abilities — clairvoyance, clairaudience, claircognizance, and clairsentience. There are branches of psychology dedicated to the study and interpretation of dreams. Notably, depth psychology is a deep dive into the subconscious and how it connects to the conscious via dreams and certain types of meditations that create a dream-like state.

Much of what we understand in modern spirituality and psychology in reference to the collective unconscious is connected to studies of the subconscious and conscious by folks such as Carl Jung and Sigmund Freud. Often, New Age spirituality uses many concepts from psychoanalysis — one of the earliest types of psychotherapy — for the purposes of healing and greater awareness/understanding of the self. While I have my reservations on some of the applications of psychoanalysis both in therapy and intuitive healing, I believe each person is the expert on how psychoanalytic concepts apply and resonate within themself.

Dream interpretation typically involves moving from the literal to the metaphorical. Setting, characters, actions, and objects — no matter how nonsensical — are all connected somehow in dreams. And there are layers to dreams, which makes dream interpretations a fun experience in expanding your curiosity.

I kept a dream journal from 2020 to 2023. There are hundreds of dreams I've recorded, and I've interpreted many but not all of them. I've learned a lot about myself, others, and my life purpose by paying attention to my dreams. I also engaged in dream-like meditations consistently for several months, which produced a lot of interesting material to work with. Here's one of those meditations.

NIGHT MEDITATION (5/25)
I saw Granny McAdams as an older yet active version of herself. She went to Springfield Baptist Church and was digging in the graveyard portion. She dug a coffin-sized hole, and I somehow ended inside of it, yet not in a dark way. I looked down, and there were some terracotta looking people below me. Then I was out of hole and was looking at Granny from a distance. There were some spirits in various stances near her. One was sitting at a desk writing or sewing something. Another one was standing a few feet away, looking like they were playing the cello or another musical instrument. They took on the appearance of black shapes — no hair, just like a minimal black body shape.

On the surface, it looks like the "dream" was just about Granny McAdams — one of my departed ancestors that I consider one of my spirit guides — at our Home Church,[1] with some spirits around her. I assumed these were other deceased ancestors she wanted me to find. Looking at things more symbolically, I knew coffins and graveyards were related to death and rebirth. The fact that I was inside of a coffin-sized hole may have meant that I was going through some kind of death and rebirth process. That was about as far as I could get with interpreting that dream at that time.

About a month later, a family friend died, and I flew out to Atlanta for her funeral. My Granny McAdams' Home Church was only about two hours away. This did not seem coincidental, so I made the drive. Of the many interesting things that happened while I was there, I found the spirits and terracotta people from the dream. They were Granny McAdams' stillborn children. There were flowers and offerings on the grave sites for others around them, but they had

---

1.   In the African American community, a Home Church is the church one attends primarily. Entire families are known to belong to one Home Church where many members are located. During family reunions, my mother's family hosts a Homecoming church service that same weekend.

none. I left sunflowers on their graves and sang a song to them. I cried on the plane ride home when I thought of them and the grief my granny must have suffered to not have these children she was preparing for in body and spirit. As someone who hasn't yet had children but wants them, I felt a bit more connected to her. I also had other experiences that were related to the death/rebirth theme while I was in the graveyard.

STEPS

1. Once you wake up from a dream or finish a particularly visual meditation, immediately make a record of it.
2. Note the setting, characters, objects, actions, and other elements you feel are important.
3. Explore the literal meaning of the elements of the dream.
4. Explore the symbolic meaning of the elements of the dream using your understanding of symbols.
5. Explore the symbolic meaning of the elements of the dream using general understandings of symbols, such as archetypes of people, places, and things.
6. Pick the elements of these explorations that resonate with you and put them together as best you can.
7. Be open to other interpretations and manifestations of dream elements in your daily life.

<u>REFLECTION</u>

1. How clear or vivid was the dream you were working with?
2. What elements were hard to interpret?
3. What elements were easy to interpret?

Balancing Act Exercise

<u>PURPOSE</u>

For this exercise, the purpose is to incorporate all the ways of knowing — authority, reason, experience, intuition, and social cognition. You will do this by naming each as a "part." This is based off a therapy model called internal family systems (IFS). The idea is that each person has different internal parts of our self that have distinct experiences and reactions to our external world. For example, as I've done my own IFS work, I've recognized that some of my internal parts are "the loner," "the dreamer," and "the teenager." These internal parts create a "family" that we can acknowledge as we live our lives.

Acknowledging these different parts can help us see that we are expansive feelings with more complex thoughts and feelings than we are sometimes reduced to. I believe the same thing is applicable to ways of knowing; I am often using multiple ways, and we don't have to silence any of them because none of them are bad or wrong.

<u>STEPS</u>

1. Identify the "authority" part of yourself. Give it a name.
2. Identify the "reason" part of yourself. Give it a name.
3. Identify the "experience" part of yourself. Give it a name.
4. Identify the "intuition" part of yourself. Give it a name.
5. Identify the "social cognition" part of yourself. Give it a name.
6. Think about a topic that feels unresolved.
7. Imagine your parts having a conversation about the topic. Make a record of the conversation.

REFLECTION

1. Which parts were easier to identify?
2. Which parts were harder to identify?
3. Which parts spoke the most?
4. Which parts did not say much?
5. Were you able to get closer to resolution with the topic? If so, what was the resolution?

PART TWO

Napping while at school

9

WHAT IS FLOWING?

As early as my freshman year of college, I have struggled with getting to bed before midnight. I was balancing school, work, and my personal life outside of my parents' home. It was not uncommon to see me up at 3 am doing homework while watching cartoons on my living room couch. I rarely scheduled classes before 10 am. The one time I had to schedule an 8 am class was brutal. I was truly a night owl.

When I got to my PhD program, my sleep really took a nosedive. During the first two years of my PhD program, I had less control over my schedule and had to work in sleeping and waking hours the best way I could. I got to the point that I would work until I felt too tired to continue, and then I would sleep. This went on for a while. Sometimes, this meant that I would fall asleep after a three-hour seminar around 4 pm, wake up at 9 pm, and then work from about midnight to 2 am.

During the third and last year of my PhD program, I learned more about my natural sleeping and waking habits. I woke up around 10 or 11 am and took my time waking up. I had breakfast and then participated in some sort of creative activity. Usually, this was painting or sketching. I then would probably do some kind of movement, if I hadn't already. I had a treadmill in my bedroom and liked walking on it while watching Marvel movies. Then, in the late afternoon or early evening, I was ready to work—like, the heavier, mentally demanding work that was my dissertation study. I could easily work from about 6 pm to midnight (with breaks) and get quite a bit done.

Knowing this about myself helped me understand why 9-5 jobs were hard for me. I had a 9-5 job during my PhD program. It was a clinical job that I didn't enjoy overall, but I really did not enjoy driving a half hour to that job every morning. I had two other 9-5 jobs after my PhD was completed. They were both paperwork-intensive, and it never felt like I was off the clock. I struggled a lot with personal time during the first job. I had more personal time while working at the second job, but I was burnt out every few months, like clockwork. My colleagues were great about trying to help me when I was burnt out since it seemed like we all experienced that from time to time, but the systems and structure of that job were not adequate when it came to therapist development or self-care.

In late 2021, I received my full licensure to practice therapy. This meant that I didn't have to have a supervisor anymore and I could practice all by myself. I quickly set up my private practice and saw my first clients in late September. Initially, I only saw clients on Saturdays. Then, once I got more clients, I added Fridays. Between my 9-5 job and my private practice, I was seeing clients 7 days a week. I was exhausted, and it was beginning to show up in my work. My caseload was more challenging at my 9-5 job, and I was starting to call in sick more due to exhaustion and migraines that started coming more frequently. I was planning on quitting my 9-5 job in mid to late 2022 so I could earn and save up money like the financial gurus were advising before switching to the entrepreneur life. I realized quickly that I would not make it that long. I put in a month's notice and was done with my 9-5 job on December 31st, 2021.

The first several weeks of 2022 were quieter than the last several years of my life. There was more time to sleep and relax, and I took advantage of that time. I woke up around 10:30 am almost every day. I read a lot of books, especially clinical ones that I didn't have the mental capacity for when I was burnt out at my last job. I made art. I cooked most of my meals. I made more time for my family and friends. I started going to the on-site gym that I had neglected for over a year since moving into my apartment complex. I built up my business. I got more clients and started seeing them on Thursdays as well as Fridays. I still went to bed well after midnight.

At the same time, I was developing my coaching and consulting services on the days I was not seeing therapy clients. It was fun, challenging work that was similar to but different from my therapy work. It tapped into my racial equity research skill set that I'd developed more in my PhD program as well as the experience I had gathered over the years advocating for racial equity in non-profit organizations. I was developing trainings, workshops, and a general framework for how I could do this work in a sustainable, collaborative way.

This was the kind of work environment I enjoyed. It was rewarding and continues to be. I still have more or less the same schedule I had when I transitioned to full-time self-employment a couple of years ago. The only exception is that now I travel more often for both business and pleasure.

I have found a good flow in my life with the different areas that matter to me, and I have not experienced burnout at all.

Flow: The Concept

Flow is a concept that has been around for a long time. It has not always been known as "flow," but many ancient peoples and spiritual traditions have acknowledged its presence. African traditional religions have rituals that put participants into a flow state via song and dance. Eastern religions have used a variety of meditative practices to help adherents get into a flow state. Early Christians used prayer and focus on religious symbols to increase focus on intentions.

In the 1970s, a man named Mihaly Csikszentmihalyi introduced the concept of flow to the field of psychology and coined the term. It represents a state of complete immersion and absorption in an activity. It often leads to peak performance and profound satisfaction.[1] Flow can also just be a space in which you are most inspired and most able to perform certain behaviors that are suited to your skill set. It's when we feel "in the zone."

Flow tends to have certain characteristics, such as clear goals and immediate feedback. It requires complete concentration on the task at hand, often a distorted sense of time, and a sense of control over the activity. Folks in their flow often report forgetting about their worries and experiencing a sense of effortlessness. There is a confidence that the

---

1. Csikszentmihalyi, M. (1990). Flow: *The psychology of optimal experience.* HarperCollins e-books.

process is moving towards a goal and that challenges presented can be overcome.[2]

Finding your flow and submitting to the process can open you up to different interests, skills, and ideas. It can help you embrace more of a multi-hyphenate life, as many creatives do. Creative insights can arise intuitively when your mind is relaxed and flowing. Artists, writers, and all types of innovators describe how they tap into intuitive sources of inspiration as they are creating. This is flow.

While in flow, folks report lower stress and anxiety levels, higher self-esteem, and an overall sense of well-being.[3] Often, people feel happy; they are open and curious. Flow can create feelings of joy. Enjoyment is about experiencing something more favorably than was expected. Flow is found at the intersection of boredom and anxiety, when challenges are balanced with the person's ability to act.[4] Without feelings of stress and insecurity, people are in a better position to explore and follow inspiration. They can find solutions to problems, build on ideas, and grow their confidence in activities. Flow can create a higher quality of life, as it promotes personal growth and self-actualization. This is how I feel with my current lifestyle.

Curious Questions

  1. Where do you find yourself able to flow?

---

2. Ibid.

3. Chen, J. H., Tsai, P. H., Lin, Y. C., Chen, C. K., & Chen, C. Y. (2019). Mindfulness training enhances flow state and mental health among baseball players in Taiwan. *Psychology Research and Behavior Management, 12,* 15–21. https://doi.org/10.2147/ PRBM.S188734

4. Csikszentmihalyi, M. (1990). Flow: *The psychology of optimal experience.* HarperCollins e-books.

2. Why might finding flow be important to the life you are creating?

3. What kind of insights have you had when in a state of flow?

4. What have you been able to create or produce while in a state of flow?

~

A watercolor portrait I painted of my cousin, Amer

10

CREATING FLOW

I wrote a lot during my PhD program, Like, *a lot.* Between writing smaller papers for classes and writing long chapters for my dissertation, there was a lot of academic writing. Academic writing, while educational and sometimes even lyrically interesting, has never been known for its creativity. It is more technical in nature, and it is more concerned with communicating clear ideas and processes than evoking emotion in the writer or reader. This isn't to say academic writing never does those things, but they are not the goal.

As you can imagine, I got pretty tired of spending so much time writing. I used to enjoy it as a creative outlet. I was doing so much of it for purposes other than my own creative satisfaction. I had to find something else to do that would satisfy my urges to create.

I'd been told a year or two earlier by a psychic that art, specifically painting, would likely be something I would enjoy. I didn't do anything with that information for a while, and then one day I decided I was going to go out and buy some alcohol markers and a sketchbook. I'd been watching

several art YouTube channels at this point and decided I was
ready to start making things myself.

After getting over the buyer's remorse of spending so
much money on markers—they were about $60—I started
to experiment. I swatched all the colors. I tried blending the
colors together. The results were sometimes beautiful,
sometimes discouraging. I started making sketches of
people and small objects. Knowing that I was nowhere near
a professional, I was happy to see my progress with
improvements in my technique over time. I began to understand the difference between highlights and shadows on top
of the base color. I knew how to create better skin tone color
combinations over time and how to make them look
warmer or cooler on the page.

Eventually, I felt brave enough to venture into watercol-
ors. I don't remember why I didn't start with a more
predictable painting medium, like acrylic, but I was probably watching watercolor artists online and wanted to try
out some of their techniques. I bought a set and some
brushes, and then I was on my way. I followed more or less
the same process I used when I was learning how to use
markers. Eventually, I was almost exclusively drawing
portraits, mostly of people in my life. Some of them looked
like the person I was drawing, some didn't. I got familiar
with the "ugly phase" of an art piece—the phase somewhere in the middle where it looks very off from what you're
trying to accomplish—and pushing through it.

I got to a place where I knew my process for painting
watercolor portraits. First, I created a preliminary sketch in
red colored pencil. I would then find the darkest areas of the
piece and outline them with black archival pen. Then, I
would lay in the skin color that would serve as the base.
This was usually the lightest color, as watercolor works best

working light to dark. I would be aware of the whitest or lightest areas of the portrait and try to avoid painting those areas to keep them white. Any base hair and clothing colors would come next. Then I would start layering in darker colors on the skin, hair, and clothing, which helped create depth in the piece. Next, I would look for the lightest areas in the portrait again and fill them in with white gel pen. These were minimal, so I wouldn't overwhelm the viewer with bright spots. I wanted to keep a balance of light and dark that created an interesting piece.

An unexpected outcome of me pursuing art at this time was that it benefitted the research and writing I was doing at school. Doing a completely different activity that engaged me visually and mentally helped me think through other things in ways I hadn't thought of before. I developed more curiosity and patience with the work I was doing on my dissertation. I wasn't thinking as technically as I was before and was able to be more creative with my ideas and felt more permission to imagine beyond what was possible.

Flow as Energy

There is a saying that "energy flows where attention goes." Many talk about attention being a type of psychic energy. Our own consciousness is considered a type of energy, along with kinetic energy and electric energy. It is considered scientific matter.[1]

We typically talk about consciousness in three ways, mostly thanks to Sigmund Freud. First is the conscious

---

1. Merriam-Webster. (n.d.). Psychic energy. In Merriam-Webster.com medical dictionary. https://www.merriam-webster.com/medical/psychic%20energy

mind, where we are actively thinking and processing information. It is also aware of self and its actions. Second is the subconscious mind, where we often have realizations about actions and reactions. This is the space where we think, "Hmm...I never made that connection before" or "I didn't realize why I did that. That makes so much sense." Dreams are often considered to be products of our subconscious working to make important life themes conscious. Finally, there is the unconscious mind. This is where our memories and deepest beliefs lie.[2]

The mind goes through cycles of active processing and resting. We can process a lot of information as humans, but we cannot process everything all the time. We need breaks.[3] Also, while we do have some control over what we focus on, some of the processes that impact our focus are subconscious or unconscious and may not be things we are aware of. We can create more awareness around where we focus our attention, which some would call being intentional. But we don't do this all the time. In fact, many people spend their free time doing things that don't require much focus or attention. We spend time on social media, streaming shows, napping, exercising, and doing other activities.[4] When we do this, we are seeking to balance out activities that require a lot of focus or attention with activities that don't require a lot of focus or attention. Flow can be found in the midst of active processing and resting through other activities.

2. Seltzer, L. F. (2019). Subconscious vs. unconscious: How to tell the difference. Psychology Today. https://www.psychologytoday.com/us/blog/evolution-the-self/ 201912/subconscious-vs-unconscious-how-tell-the-difference

3. Pillay, S. (2017). Secret to brain success: Intelligent cognitive rest. Harvard University. https://www.health.harvard.edu/blog/secret-to-brain-success-intelligent- cognitive-rest-2017050411705

4. I recognize some levels of these activities can require more focus; I am referring to less intense forms of them.

Circumstances of Flow

There is some evidence of characteristics that are found in the flow state. Based on studies of the flow state, here is what has generally emerged.[5]

1. *Clear goals are usually identified.* There are typically goals or intentions that you care about whether they are big or small. You are aware of these goals in your conscious mind.
2. *There is the possibility of completion of these goals.* Based on your skill set, you feel like you are able to complete your goals.
3. *An element of concentration tends to be part of the process.* You are focused on your goals and accomplishing them.
4. *Usually, there is immediate feedback during the process, which can guide behavior.* If you are seeing progress often towards your goal during the activity, you will be more likely to continue doing it and staying in the flow.
5. *There is a sense of deep, yet effortless involvement in the activity.* This may also be a result of your skill set and your ability to follow through with the activity. It doesn't feel too hard, but there is still enough challenge to keep you engaged.
6. *Folks feel a sense of control.* External factors do not distract you or seem to have much of a role while you are immersed in the activity.
7. *The sense of self often disappears.* This is the space

5. Csikszentmihalyi, M. (1990). *Flow: The psychology of optimal experience.* HarperCollins e-books.

where you feel as if you have "become one" with
the activity.

8. *Time feels like it is altered or distorted.* You may feel
   like you've been spending hours on the activity
   when it has only been a few minutes. On the
   other hand, hours have passed when it feels like
   it's only been minutes since you started the
   activity.

Ways to Create Flow

People create and experience flow in a variety of ways. I'll
talk about a few here and invite you to consider others that
haven't been mentioned. Gameplay is one way that folks get
into a flow state.[6] Different types of games exist that satisfy
the desire to achieve goals and feel success. In fact, the
games clearly lay out the goals you are to accomplish. Role-
playing games put us in another world where we have
control over what happens to some extent, as if we were the
main characters. Strategy games encourage us to think
before we act and predict outcomes. Action games excite
our senses and provide thrills, usually at a quicker pace
than other games. Puzzles give our brains a fun tingle as we
try to solve the problems the puzzles present.

Creating and consuming art can activate different parts
of your brain and allow them to flow together. Creating[7] art,
like visual art and music, taps into both parts of the brain to

6.   Wittmann, M. (2021). Time speeds up in flow states when playing video
games. Psychology Today. https://www.psychologytoday.com/us/blog/sense-
time/202105/ time-speeds-in-flow-states-when-playing-video-games

7.   Gharib, M. (2020). Feeling artsy? Here's how making art helps your
brain. National Public Radio. https://www.npr.org/sections/health-shots/
2020/01/11/795010044/ feeling-artsy-heres-how-making-art-helps-your-brain

access both creativity—the inspiration out into action—and the science, the process. Once inspiration hits, you may follow it and have a conscious or unconscious process that you tap into in order to express your original ideas.

Meditation can create flow fairly easily for some folks. It calms parts of the nervous system and allows for thoughts and feelings to flow more effortlessly.[8] Engaging in rituals can be meditative for many people. Rituals include activities like prayer, reading or reciting mantras, singing, sitting and reflecting, and taking nature walks. They can be anything that you do over and over that creates a "second nature" way of doing things. When you are doing something you are used to, you can allow the brain to do other things rather than focus so much on the details of the ritual.

Speaking of taking a walk, other types of physical activities can put you into a flow state. Many[9] find asanas, a physical manifestation of yoga, to be very helpful. In fact, a series of asanas done together is called a "flow." Additionally, activities like running, dancing, and martial arts can help folks feel like they are "in the zone."

One more way of creating flow is via plant medicine. Similar to other medicines, plant medicine can help remove mental and physical blockages, therefore facilitating flow.[10] Similar to prescription medication, plant medicine can have different effects on the body depending on the plant itself

8. Rutledge, T. (2019). How meditation improves emotional and physical health. Psychology Today. https://www.psychologytoday.com/us/blog/the-healthy-journey/ 201908/how-meditation-improves-emotional-and-physical-health

9. Csikszentmihalyi, M. (1990). *Flow: The psychology of optimal experience.* HarperCollins e-books.

10. National Academies of Sciences, Engineering, and Medicine; Health and Medicine Division. (2017). Therapeutic effects of cannabis and cannabinoids. https:// www.ncbi.nlm.nih.gov/books/NBK425767/

and your unique body composition.[11] Some plants are better for their calming properties and others are better for experiencing hallucinations that can be deeply inspiring. Plants like psilocybin, a mushroom, are being researched more now as a supplement to already approved therapies like cognitive-behavioral therapy.[12] Many herbal remedies are legal, though many psychedelics are illegal for the general public in the United States.

Collaborative Flowing

While it is possible for us to get into the flow as individuals, it is also possible for us to experience the flow state with others. This is called synergy, which is the combination of forces to create a larger effect. It is the embodiment of the sum being greater than its parts. The energy of flow synchronized is how I like to see it. Synergetic flow, collaborative flow is what drives me to do the work of healing in the way I do. When I am in the therapy room with groups of people, I am looking for the moments when people come together and are curious. When they are open to understanding each other. When they find common ground, even in their differences, and can work towards goals that strengthen their relationships.

What I also enjoy is the collaborative flowing itself. Some groups do not really need solutions—and often there

11. Tersavich, C. (2022). Psychedelics vs. plant medicines: Definitions and differences. Mindbloom. https://www.mindbloom.com/blog/psychedelics-vs-plant-medicines- definitions-differences

12. Yaden, D. B., Earp, D., Graziosi, M., Friedman-Wheeler, D., Luoma, J. B., & Johnson, M. W. (2022). Psychedelics and Psychotherapy: Cognitive-Behavioral Approaches as Default. *Frontiers in psychology, 13,* 873279. https://doi.org/10.3389/ fpsyg.2022.873279

aren't concrete ones that everyone agrees on—but a sense of validation and feeling of belonging. This departure from solution-focused interventions can be hard for some to embrace, especially in more institutionalized settings that feel like they must "fix" everything that seems to be a problem. Flow-finding interventions can create a strong sense of belonging in groups because each person has their own contribution to the conversation and feels engaged in the overall direction of it.

I find this in my consulting work often when I am helping groups build psychological safety with each other. This is especially important for team members to feel safe with their leaders, and it can take several interactions that demonstrate safety for folks to really relax and share their questions, concerns, and innovative ideas. There can eventually evolve a flow in these interactions that feels good and is sought out. Flow becomes an end in and of itself.

Let's take the example of a team I've worked with several times. We will use the circumstances of flow mentioned earlier to demonstrate how this team fell into a collaborative flow.

1. *Clear goals were identified.* At first, the team had clear objectives to learn about psychological safety. I gave them a lot of content, including working definitions and skills to practice. Eventually, we moved on to practicing the skills more heavily. In these latter sessions, I encouraged them to focus less on concrete goals and more on the flow that could be found in the practice of psychological safety. They were doing more of the talking to each other, rather than me talking to them.

2. *The goals felt possible.* Every session had 1-2 goals to pay attention to, and they were simple. This led to the increased possibility of success in achieving them. Based on their feedback, it sounds like the goals felt more and more possible as the sessions went on and they felt more capable with the practice of psychological safety.

3. *Concentration was part of the process.* Again, I shared a lot of information with them to ponder and digest. They were eager students and worked to understand how to develop increased psychological safety on the team.

4. *There was immediate feedback during the process.* As the team learned about psychological safety, they asked questions, which I answered promptly. They responded favorably to the examples I provided to solidify concepts. They gave feedback to team leads at the end of each session and identified what they wanted to work on in future sessions, which I incorporated. This increased their engagement and ability to get into collaborative flow more quickly.

5. *There was deep, yet effortless involvement in the activity.* As the team talked more with each other in both small groups and large groups, they were deeply engaged in the activity and had profound revelations about themselves. Because we were using formats they identified as being enjoyable, this likely contributed to feelings of effortlessness.

6. *Folks felt a sense of control.* Because the team leads and I consulted team members about what they wanted, they felt a sense of control over the

direction of the individual sessions and the overall work we were doing to cultivate a stronger sense of psychological safety.

7. *The sense of self disappeared.* Now, this one I'm not sure about. I feel like everyone remained self-aware in the process. But maybe they would say differently.

8. *Time felt like it was altered or distorted.* Every session, team members would comment that it felt like there was not enough time to get to everything. This was after a 3-hour session! Over time, we learned to incorporate more breaks and plan for a longer session time to make sure we could process what we learned together.

Curious Questions

1. How do you experience a flow state?
2. Where have you noticed flow most in your life?
3. How do you experience flow with others?

Reflecting in the Blue Ridge Mountains

11

BARRIERS TO FLOW

Many of my career experiences after my master's degree were not conducive to my flow experience. I started most of them being optimistic that I would be embraced and then discovered within several weeks that things were not as they were advertised during the interview process. I found myself in spaces that did not value creativity and innovation as much as they said they did. When I brought up questions or concerns, I was often dismissed. Expectations for my roles were unrealistic; they were not grounded in reality. I often had supervisors and managers who were too far removed from being "on the ground" with the folks who were doing the most client-facing work.

After completing my PhD, I was exhausted. It took me 3 years what takes the average PhD student around 8 years to do. I was not only burnt out from the work I had done, but also by the administrative culture of the program. I knew I did not want to be in academia to be part of the abuse cycle that PhD students—especially BIPOC—are often put through in order to be considered doctors. It was what is called an "invalidating environment," according to dialectical behavioral therapy.

I didn't have success with my job hunt for several months. I was about to stop trying and move back to Utah when I got a call back for a clinical position in the area. The job was with a smaller mental health agency that had locations across the state. It was Black-owned, and most of my colleagues were Black, which felt very affirming for me. It was the type of environment I wanted to be in after being in many white-led organizations. The interview process felt affirming, and I liked the folks I saw in leadership — again, mostly Black.

Things turned sour fairly quickly. There was a patriarchal culture that permeated the company. The boss was always considered to be right and making him happy was the most important thing. Fear was often used as a tactic to get employees to be productive. There was a general resistance by him and the rest of the company to my initial empathic, curious style of leadership. He told me he tried that in the past and that it didn't work. I tried his more fear-based approach and that not only backfired, but damaged some relationships with my supervisees.

I learned that the CEO had a lot of leadership red flags. Sometimes, I was praised by him, and other times, he disparaged me and others when he was unhappy. When he felt threatened by me, he would find ways to gaslight me to invalidate either my accuracy in assessing a situation or my general success. It seemed like he took turns with who would be the target of his anger. I took the placating route with him at times just so I could do my job and not be harassed by him.

The CEO was unkind to many of his female employees. He spoke ill of some of them, and I often advocated for them. Sometimes, he publicly humiliated them during meetings, and I told him that was unnecessary. Once, I was pulled into his office with another male leader and was told to temper myself because women weren't meant to be leaders the way men were. Women were better seen and not heard. The CEO also threatened to fire me for sticking up for a member of the leadership team once, which made me laugh on the inside because my salary and benefits at that job were a joke. He only had to do that to me once, and I turned in my two weeks' notice.

I was overworked, underpaid, and made to believe that my approaches couldn't be as good as the CEO's. Leaving that job and that area was like a breath of fresh air because I felt like I could finally go back to being myself again. I found work that was more meaningful and helped me reach more of my larger goals. They paid me better, too, and I found colleagues who have been better friends with better boundaries. I was closer to getting back into a flow that served me.

Stress and Trauma

The flow state is impacted by different levels of stress and trauma. Stress is mental strain that results from our skill set not being able to manage an event effectively. A great example of this would be the COVID-19 pandemic that threw individuals, communities, and the world at large into a frenzy. We know that there were higher levels of stress, depression, and anxiety across age groups, racial groups, and genders.[1] Stress can be short-term or long-term,

---

1. Manchia, M., Gathier, A. W., Yapici-Eser, H., Schmidt, M. V., de Quervain, D., van Amelsvoort, T., Bisson, J. I., Cryan, J. F., Howes, O. D., Pinto, L., van der Wee, N. J., Domschke, K., Branchi, I., & Vinkers, C. H. (2022). The impact of the prolonged COVID-19 pandemic on stress resilience and

depending on the activity. Often, we are dealing with daily stresses that can have a small impact on us. On the other hand, more demanding jobs, such as those in healthcare, can be more stressful. Life transitions can be more stressful until we find a new normal or a routine that reduces the level of stress.

Additionally, the pandemic was a traumatizing experience for many. Trauma is a psychological response to a single or repeated deeply distressing event that has long-term effects. In this way, trauma goes deeper than typical stresses that we encounter. Trauma is a full-brain and full-body experience. What I mean by that is we have many ways mentally, emotionally, physically, socially, and spiritually that trauma impacts us. Some of these ways are conscious, but many are unconscious. Research has been done on adverse childhood experiences (ACEs), which are understood to be potentially traumatic experiences that impact cognitive development.[2] Those with a higher ACE score are likely to struggle more at school, at work, and in relationships with others. Traumatic brain injuries (TBIs) can change how the brain functions long-term.[3] Many have talked about how after a TBI, their lives changed dramatically, and they were no longer the person they were prior to their injury.

mental health: A critical review across waves. *European neuropsychopharmacology : the journal of the European College of Neuropsychopharmacology, 55*, 22–83. https://doi.org/10.1016/ j.euroneuro.2021.10.864

2. Centers For Disease Control and Prevention. (2023). Adverse Childhood Experiences   (ACEs).   https://www.cdc.gov/violenceprevention/aces/index.html

3. National Institute of Neurological Disorders and Stroke. (2023). Traumatic Brain Injury (TBI).
      https://www.ninds.nih.gov/health-information/disorders/traumatic-brain-injury-   tbi#:~:text=Some%20types%20of%20TBI%20can,permanent%20disability%2C%20an d%20even%20death.

BIPOC experience many traumas at many levels. We have the unique addition of racial trauma, as well, which is largely felt but often dismissed by the very institutions we rely on for survival, such as the education system,[4] legal system[5], and healthcare system.[6] Racial trauma resulting from workplace discrimination is also becoming more visible.[7] With all of these compounded traumas, it may be hard to recognize what a clear and focused flow may feel like consistently.

While it is clear how stress and trauma can block flow, they can also create flow for some people. There is plenty of evidence of folks under pressure or being oppressed expressing high levels of creativity. For Black people with a history of enslavement, there is a long-standing tradition of using music and dance as a means of survival. Negro spirituals, sung by African Americans, included messages of freedom, including routes to escape north. There is speculation that capoeira, a type of martial art with Afro-Brazilian origins, developed over time to look like an intricate dance in order to look less threatening to colonizers rather than a fighting style.

4. McAdoo, G., Williams, K., & Howard, T. C. (2023). Racially Just, Trauma-Informed Care for Black Students. *Urban Education, 0*(0). https://doi.org/10.1177/00420859231175668

5. Slovinsky, T.L. (2023). The thread of trauma: A critical analysis of the criminal legal system. *Social Sciences, 12*(9): 467. https://doi.org/10.3390/socsci12090467

6. Ruqaiijah, Y., Clark, B., & Figueroa, J. F. (2022). Structural racism in historical and modern US health care policy. *Health Affairs, 41*(2). https://doi.org/10.1377/ hlthaff.2021.01466

7. Next Big Idea Club. (2022). 5 key insights on racial trauma in the workplace. Fast Company & Inc. https://www.fastcompany.com/90717059/5-key-insights-on-racial- trauma-in-the-workplaceFast Company & Inc.

Other Barriers to Flow

There are other ways that flow can be blocked. Let's look at the characteristics found in the flow state, as mentioned in the last chapter. But let's invert them.

1. *Unclear goals.* Without goals that are identified, there can be no sense of achievement. I do not think all goals must be completely conscious or the sole focus of an activity, but if it feels like we are not moving towards a goal, no matter how general, we can become confused, frustrated, or unsatisfied.

2. *Impossibility of completion.* The image of a hamster running on a wheel comes to mind. If we feel like we are being set up for failure, we can burn out trying to make something work that isn't possible.

3. *Delayed feedback or none at all.* If we are running an app on a device and it suddenly stops working, we usually do whatever we can to get it working again. We want the process to continue uninterrupted, especially if we were working on something important to us. The app is responding to us, which is feedback, and when it stops working so immediately, we feel interrupted in our flow. It may take time to get back into it, depending on how long it takes to get back into that quicker feedback loop of us doing an action and the app responding to the action.

4. *Superficial amount or demanding amount of effort needed.* Many people become easily bored by

busy work. If an activity feels superficial or meaningless, interest can be lost. On the other hand, if the task requires more effort than our skill set can handle, this can create feelings of anxiety and frustration rather than joy.

5. *Lack of control.* When it feels like we do not have a say in how we perform an activity or even the activities we participate in, we may not feel connected to the activity. Also, elements that are out of our control can be more unpredictable than we can handle, which can bring unpleasant feelings during the experience. When we are in environments that do not seem to fit our flow, this can also feel like a lack of control. These spaces don't encourage your talents and skills, or they may not provide enough challenge or intrigue.

6. *Self-consciousness.* When we are too aware of ourselves and how we are experiencing an activity, this can separate us from the flow we are trying to achieve while doing the activity. Also, a lot of self-consciousness can lead to self-criticism.

7. *Fixation on time.* When our eyes are trained on the clock, we can disconnect from our flow experience easily. Some folks notice that constantly looking at watches and phones can create pressure to move more quickly or slowly rather than allowing the natural passage of time to occur. When we are fixed on time, we lack presence with the activity at hand.

Decolonizing Flow

Since we have talked about decolonizing knowledge, let's chat a bit about decolonizing flow. I have been exposed to different ways of looking at why people experience psychological blockages, especially from a psychotherapy perspective. I have also been exposed to several spiritual perspectives, and there is some overlap. What I've seen is that many individualistic, Western ways of looking at blockages are based on our internal workings. Basically, if we change our internal experience by changing our mindset, our blockages will go away, and we will be able to flow better.

In psychotherapy, this is found in models such as cognitive-behavioral therapy (CBT). This model suggests that we all have errors in our thinking that we need to be aware of and question rather than accept at face value.[8] Another popular therapy model that focuses more on our thoughts and memory is eye movement desensitization and reprocessing (EMDR). EMDR has been a breakthrough trauma therapy that has helped many people process situations like sexual abuse and childhood trauma.[9] However, both CBT and EMDR by themselves do not target the external experiences we encounter every day. As a Black woman, these therapies by themselves will not protect me from the varying levels of racism and sexism I experience frequently. I may have skills to reduce the effect they have on me, but

8. American Psychological Association. (2017). What is cognitive behavioral therapy? https://www.apa.org/ptsd-guideline/patients-and-families/cognitive-behavioral

9. American Psychological Association. (2017). "Eye Movement Desensitization and Reprocessing (EMDR) therapy." https://www.apa.org/ptsd-guideline/treatments/eye- movement-reprocessing

they do nothing to directly address changes at a familial, community, or societal level.

My Mormon upbringing also had a strong mental component to its spirituality. I was taught to "pray always," which essentially was a way to keep me thinking positively. I was taught a gospel of prosperity, which meant that as long as I was thinking and doing things the Lord would approve of, I would receive blessings upon blessings. On my mission, for example, a popular saying was that the more difficult the challenges I endured, the more attractive my husband would be. To date, I'm still one of the only missionaries from my area that remains unmarried 12 years after returning home. Simply being optimistic and working hard did not bring me a husband at all, let alone an attractive one. Some would say, "It just hasn't happened yet, but it's coming." While that has been true at times, there have been countless times in my life when something I felt was promised or at least certain did not happen in a specified time frame or at all. Simply being a good person does not mean good things always happen to you because you want them, and this perspective negates the privileges and oppressions that people experience.

With my Mormon-adjacent psychotherapy clients, I notice how this focus on thoughts can create obsessions with doing the right thing at all times. Clients with high anxiety and obsessive-compulsive behaviors often tell me about how they stressed over their thought patterns as children in order to not be disobedient to God. This carries into how they approach life now, whether they are still participating in that same spiritual practice or not. Trying to think positively continuously did not help them; it did the opposite and harmed them.

Interestingly, when I started looking into New Age spirituality in graduate school, I found similar rhetoric around positive thinking. If I would just set intentions for what I wanted for my life and aligned with the right vibration, I could manifest anything I wanted. Growth and development could be achieved personally, which was a helpful philosophy for me in many ways. This view of manifestation was a common idea I found from practitioners across racial and ethnic lines.

At first, I thought maybe this was something ancestral found in a lot of different indigenous spiritual practices. What I found over time, however, was that the New Age/New Thought movement, which has European origins and is very much individualistic in nature, was responsible for the popularity of manifestation.[10] As I've looked more into African Traditional Religions and other indigenous spiritual practices, there are similar ideas to manifestation, but there are often caveats and acknowledgement of other energies that may work with or against you. The latter emphasizes prioritizing community and being part of one to help you connect more with the collective and nature. There has been quite a bit of criticism of New Age spirituality by pagan and indigenous spiritual communities for essentially sampling a bunch of spiritual ideas from different cultures without being rooted in any of them enough to understand or practice them effectively.

While there is a lot of benefit to looking internally to see where shifts can be made, we need to also look at the external. While race, gender, class, and other identities are socially constructed, they have very real impacts on people.

---

10. Atkinson W. W. (1906). *Thought vibration: Or, the law of attraction in the thought world.* The New Thought. http://infositelinks.com/Free/2011/12/ Thought- Vibration.pdf

It's easy for people with many privileged identities to default to the "everything is a social construct, so none of these constructs are real" argument. But if you talk to people from the most marginalized identities, you will hear stories of exclusion that lead to distress.

When looking at barriers to flow and addressing them, using methods that target our families, communities, and larger systems — in addition to the individual — can be much more effective. Additionally, focusing on the body and not just the mind has been great for helping folks move through trauma. There is more research that somatic therapies help us get in tune with our emotion center instead of trying to bypass it by trying to change our thoughts.[11] Breathwork, muscle relaxation, and exercises that increase our felt sense within the body are essential for many folks to feel like healing is happening. BIPOC communities tend to use somatic practices for healing, such as singing, dancing, and other types of rhythm-making. We heal in groups to support each other often. This helps us to find our individual and collective flow.

Regaining Flow

If you find yourself coming up against barriers to flow, there are several ways to regain the sense of it. My first suggestion would be to revisit the previous chapter, as there are several methods mentioned that can help create flow. Second, I would invite you to look at some of the techniques mentioned in the previous paragraph related to reclaiming

11. Kuhfuß, M., Maldei, T., Hetmanek, A., & Baumann, N. (2021). Somatic experiencing - effectiveness and key factors of a body-oriented trauma therapy: a scoping literature review. European *Journal of Psychotraumatology*, *12*(1), 1929023. https://doi.org/ 10.1080/20008198.2021.1929023

both somatic and collective flow practices. In addition to using these to break through barriers, here are other ways to regain a sense of flow.

1. *Do something different to change the energy.* Sometimes, when we are feeling stuck, it is an indicator that we need to switch up the activity we're engaged in. If you are reading and find yourself going over the same sentence over and over, take a walk or drink a glass of water. Watch a video. Do something that takes you out of the stuck energy and introduces new stimuli, no matter how small.

2. *Spend time with nature.* A popular phrase these days is "touch grass." This generally means to ground yourself by using your senses to connect with something tangible. Not everybody has access to grass year-round, but you may have trees or other plants you can smell or touch. Listen to the birds and other animals outside. Go for a walk around or swim in a body of water. Even looking at a picture of a landscape you love can be very peaceful and bring calm.

3. *Cleanse your space.* Whether it is your bedroom, the kitchen, or even an outdoor space, cleaning an area can also cleanse the mind in many cases. You can physically clean dirty areas. You can also metaphysically cleanse areas by using herbs, candles, water, crystals, and other items relevant to you and how you determine things are cleansed.

4. *Talk with someone.* Sometimes, talking through things with someone else can alleviate feelings of

stuckness. You can talk to a trusted loved one about what your are experiencing. If you sense that what you are experiencing is bigger than a few conversations with a friend can help you with, talking to a trusted professional like a therapist, coach, or spiritual healer could be helpful to help you move through your blockages.

Curious Questions

1. How did Niecie's environment in her shared personal experience block her flow?
2. When have you had experiences where you struggled to flow?
3. What circumstances typically block your flow?

12

EXPERIMENTS IN FLOW

The following exercises are short experiments in finding your flow and leaning into it. They align with the knowing exercises in some ways. Try them out and see what happens.

Time Tracking Exercise

<u>PURPOSE</u>

For this exercise, you will focus on how you use your time. Hopefully, you will see which activities help put you in a flow state and which do not. You may find that elements of your current routine are not conducive to flow.

<u>STEPS</u>

1. Create or find blank daily planner pages with time blocked out in 30-minute increments.
2. For a week, fill in what you did during each half hour increment.
3. After a week, look at the patterns of how you used your time.

REFLECTION

1. What activities did you enjoy the most?
2. Which activities did you enjoy the least?
3. Which activities felt the easiest to complete?
4. Which activities felt the most difficult to complete?

Breathwork Exercise

PURPOSE

Breathwork is a collection of breathing methods that have many physical and mental health benefits. It can reduce stress, improve mental clarity, relax the body, and improve blood circulation. Breathwork is a way to remove barriers to flow and open yourself up. The following excerpt is from a breathwork session that I combined with a color meditation. I made some color cards from Pantone postcards and picked one color a day to work on until I'd made it through all 100 colors in the set.

DAY MEDITATION (3/1)

using pink as a color for visualization, I pictured a lot of pink movement around me in bounces and swirls. I then saw myself wrapped in a pink blanket, which turned out to be petals of a pink flower. I was snug in there with my eyes closed, and I looked happy. There was a key with a heart on the end of it in there with me. There was pink movement around me outside of the flower as I zoomed out of the close-up on me content in the flower. Everything felt happy and utopian.

This meditation ended up becoming a staple grounding meditation for recognizing when I feel safe. I have since found a few real-life situations that bring up the strong peaceful feelings this meditation brought me.

<u>STEPS</u>

1. Find a comfortable spot, either sitting or lying down.
2. Breathe normally for a minute or so.
3. Start to take deep breaths, allowing your stomach to rise with each inhale and fall with each exhale.
4. When you have settled into this breathing pattern, start to breathe in for 4 seconds, hold the breath for 4 seconds, and then release for 4 seconds. Do this for several minutes.
5. Return to a regular breathing pattern.
6. Visualize a color you have either pre-selected or chosen at this moment.
7. Pay attention to what other visuals come to you guided by this color.

<u>REFLECTION</u>

1. How would you describe your experience with this activity?
2. Was it easy or challenging to focus?
3. What sort of images came to mind during the color meditation?
4. What other thoughts or feelings did you have during the exercise?

Hobbying Exercise

<u>PURPOSE</u>

This exercise is simple; it's all about connecting to something you enjoy that is not connected to your regular work activities. It is about connecting to something not pertinent to your survival and giving yourself permission to explore other parts of yourself.

<u>STEPS</u>

1. Pick an activity that you have enjoyed in the past or that you have been wanting to try.
2. Research the activity and what types of resources are needed to complete it.
3. Gather the necessary resources for the activity. If you don't have access to all the resources, get creative with it.

4. Do the activity. Then do it again. And then again. Make it part of your life for as long as it brings you joy.

REFLECTION

1. What hobby did you choose?
2. What drew you to this hobby initially?
3. How did you feel the first time you engaged in this hobby?
4. How did you feel after engaging in this hobby several times?

PART THREE

Family Map

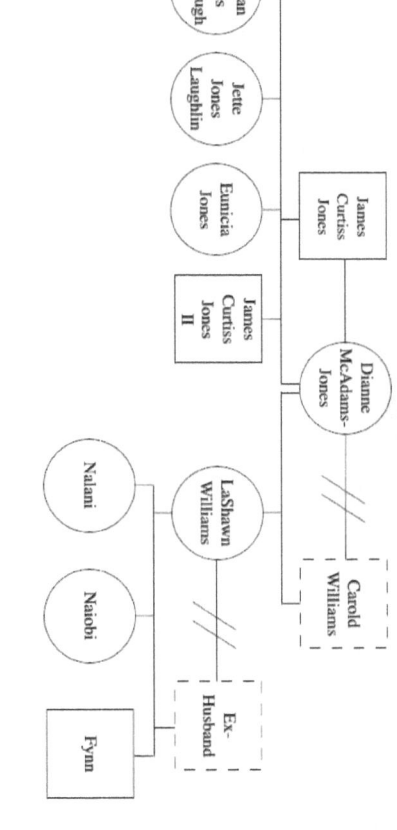

Key

□ Male
○ Female
—— Family Relationship
—⫽— Divorce
········· Not Interviewed

13

WHO IS MY FAMILY?

I know we are trying to steer away from using terms like "magical" when talking about the humanity of Black people, but I ask you to make an exception for this chapter. I think there *is* something magical about my family. The more I have learned about my family, the more I am convinced they not only have physical wonders, but metaphysical energies that have guided them to and through all kinds of circumstances. Doing my own ancestral work over the years has only strengthened this belief. It is what has driven me to work on this book. There are histories known and unknown that have left an impact on our genetics. As a family, we are holding the joy and pain of those who came before us. I know we are living out the dreams they kept, their visions for the future. For them, we are the Afrofuture.

My father, James Curtiss Jones, was born in 1943 in Dillon, South Carolina, to Samuel Jones and Eunice Mallett. He and his brothers grew up primarily with their mother, as their father died in his 30s. My father was just a young teen during this difficult period for his family. His mother—my grandmother—had to raise these boys on a schoolteacher's salary. My dad attended Morehouse College—a historically Black college/university (HBCU) for Black men in Atlanta, Georgia—for his bachelor's degree. He then attended medical school at the University of California, San Francisco campus. My dad joined the United States military, serving in the Air Force first and then the Army. It was during one of his positions overseas in Germany that he met my mother, an army nurse.

Dianne McAdams was born in 1952 in Antreville, South Carolina, to Amer Lee Sullivan and John McAdams. She grew up on a farm with her 7 siblings. Early on, her mother taught her the importance of education for a better life. As educational equity became more of a social issue, my mom became one of the first Black students to integrate her high school. She was bullied on the bus to and from her school and called derogatory names often. Mom attended Tuskegee Institute—an HBCU in Montgomery, Alabama— and got her bachelor's degree in nursing. She joined the army as a nurse. Mom married a man named Carold Williams, and they had a daughter—my sister, LaShawn. That marriage did not last, and she got divorced. In her quest for purpose, she discovered the LDS Church through a colleague. She went to a sacrament service and immediately felt at home. She decided to join the church.

During this time, my mom and dad met and dated for a few years in different geographic locations. Eventually, they got married in the United States, and my mom retired from the army so she could have and raise kids in a fairly stable environment. My family would never go overseas again for the military. My mom gave birth to my brother, James, in 1987. I came along not long after, in 1989. We were both born near Tacoma, Washington, on the local army base. We moved to San Francisco, California, a couple of years later. From there, we moved to San Antonio, Texas, where my sister, Jette, was born.

From there, we moved to Fayetteville, North Carolina. We lived at Fort Bragg, where I have the most vivid memories of childhood in the military. This is where my youngest sister, Morgan, was born. Dad retired from the army, and we stayed in the city for a while. All of us were enrolled in dance classes, and one of my favorite memories is a trio dance that LaShawn, James, and I did to Crystal Waters' 90s hit "100% Pure Love." LaShawn graduated high school and went off to Duke University in Durham.

We moved to Pennsylvania in 1999, and LaShawn moved up there, too, once she finished her bachelor's degree. James graduated high school several years later, in 2004. He was going to start school at BYU at 16 years old since he was a child genius who skipped 4th grade. My mom decided we were all going to move to Utah to be near him. Everyone except my dad knew about the move. My parents had been going through a rough patch in their marriage for a few years, and my mom was ready to start the next chapter of our family, with or without him. And we were all on board. So, we moved, and my dad ended up moving out there with us a year or two later.

LaShawn moved out there, too, partially because she'd been dating someone in New Mexico. She got married and had three kids: Fynn (also known as Becton), Naiobi (Nobi), and Nalani (Nala). My siblings and I took turns watching the kids as we were going through high school and college. Now, Fynn is in high school, and we are—as the kids say— "screaming, crying, throwing up."

In the following pages, you will read excerpts from interviews with everyone mentioned here. You will learn about how they know and how they flow. You'll see what they have done with this knowing and flowing. But first, let's talk about identity and how that showed up in the interviews.

Age

It was pretty clear to me during the interviews that there were some generational differences in how my family members understood things. My father, the oldest member of my family and sole member of the silent generation, had few words to share compared to the rest of my family members. For him, certain ideas required little elaboration. My mom, on the other hand, had a lot to say about knowing and flowing. She was the first to talk about the impact of socialization on her life. It still influences so much of how she moves through the world. As someone who came of age during integration in the South, it makes sense she would reflect heavily on racial socialization. Her psychological and maybe even literal livelihood depended on her ability to conform to white societal expectations when necessary. Paying attention to authority was also likely important to my parents, since they both came from generations that focused more on accepted authorities, though my mom deviated from the acceptance of authority outright more than my dad seemed to.

My sister, LaShawn, typifies the Gen X stereotype of the rebel and skeptic. In her responses, I heard the adamant rejection of authority as knowledge at face value. Gen X received a lot of grief for being cynical, for being slackers when they were coming of age. While some studies affirmed the higher levels of cynicism in Gen Xers, this also may have been due to the time they grew up in, as folks from older generations were also showing higher than normal levels of cynicism in the 1990s.[1] Gen X grew up in the post-civil rights era and were the beneficiaries of new legislation that granted more liberties for women, BIPOC, and other marginalized identities. LaShawn likely felt less pressure to assimilate to white American norms the way my parents did. I saw this often growing up as she questioned things and spoke out about what she did and did not agree with. She dissented and called out inconsistencies.

My siblings James, Jette, and Morgan are all millennials like me. We were all born between 1987 and 1995. Our generation is known as being more interested in psychological well-being, such as self-care, than previous generations. We are a "feelings generation" that at times gets teased for our soft skills and apparently "thin skin." We grew up in a time when sexual harassment, bullying, and other abusive behaviors were being targeted to raise healthier, well-adjusted children. As such, my siblings seemed to talk more in their interviews about things that feel good and have meaning to them at their current ages in ways my mom and LaShawn seem to lean more into now. Our generation is more focused on thriving rather than surviving, which may explain how we tap into the flow state.

Fynn and Naiobi come from Gen Z; they are both teenagers. Gen Z is known in some ways for being the conflict-avoidant or "cancel culture" generation, partly due to them growing up in a time of short-form social media content and ever-changing trends in pop culture. They are also significantly more aware of pop culture shifts and current events, which Fynn brought up as he mentioned the

---

1. See the relevant data cited in the General Social Survey by the National Opinion Research Center. This study is ongoing and has a lot of information on trends throughout the years.

current iteration of the Israel-Palestine conflict and how to support Palestinians as Americans. While I had a general understanding of current events at their age, I really only watched the news or read articles online; I didn't have access to millions of TikToks on a single topic recorded by peers around my age and around the world. These are some of their authorities—folks with lived experiences they don't have about topics that matter to them. They truly have the world at their fingertips, and I'm surprised sometimes by the thoughtful opinions they share on hot topics.

Nalani is from Gen Alpha, our kiddos in elementary school and younger. She is part of the "iPad generation," and she's honestly more tech-savvy than I am sometimes. Her understanding of the world is currently shaped by what she is learning from folks older than her. Her knowledge is mostly authority-driven. This is similar to what most of my siblings and I experienced at her age, and a lot of this knowledge by authority was around religion. At the same time, she's in a period of cognitive development that is helping her to use her reasoning skills more.

Disability

When you look at all of my family members, we are able-bodied. We don't appear to have any visible disabilities. Growing up, we were always encouraged to give gratitude that all of our limbs functioned properly, save for temporary impairments or illness. I learned later that LaShawn was partially deaf in one ear, which disqualified her from being able to join the military when she was younger.

I now have 3 siblings diagnosed with attention-deficit hyperactivity disorder (ADHD). This is considered a disability by the Americans with Disabilities Act (ADA) due to its impact on mental and physical functioning. This is significant because in my family, academic excellence is seen as a way to earn value and increase our worth in the eyes of larger society. My mom was very involved in our academic lives as kids and worked to help us however she could, so we could do well in school. She openly said she did not believe in ADD—a narrow, outdated term to refer to what we now understand to be ADHD. I noticed a difference in how I was treated compared to some of my siblings with school performance. I was often praised for receiving high marks and my study habits. Some of my siblings were called lazy and ableist slurs when they didn't perform the way they were expected to. This extended outside of school to organization and cleanliness around the house.

I think this harmful treatment had a stronger impact on some of my siblings more than others. Morgan was the first to officially get diagnosed with ADHD, and this was while she was young and living at home. James and LaShawn only recently got diagnosed in the last couple of years, well into adulthood. I think about how this has impacted how they navigate the world now. If this had been understood and accepted when they were younger, I wonder how their upbringing and understanding of themselves would be different.

As I think about Fynn and Nalani, it appears that their ADHD symptoms have been caught early enough that their lives could turn out differently than that of my siblings with ADHD. While not officially diagnosed, Fynn and Nalani may be in what some experts call the "subclinical" range of presentation, which means they present many symptoms but don't quite meet the full criteria of diagnosis. They also could be in the clinical range and just don't know it yet; they haven't been tested. But to have a mom who readily recognizes what they are struggling with and validates it while they are young hopefully helps them navigate those struggles while acknowledging and encouraging their already-present strengths and skills.

Religion & Spirituality

Religion is a core theme in my family, though not everyone identifies as being religious. My parents grew up in Christian families, my siblings and I grew up in a Christian home, and my nieces and nephew are being raised in Christian homes. Interestingly, my parents grew up in the Black Church tradition, while my siblings and I did not since we were raised Mormon. Our beliefs and practices around religion have some similarities and differences. It seems like there may have been more of a rigid adherence to religious doctrine when my siblings and I were younger that has become more flexible over time. Part of that has to do with us being older, but I believe generational shifts in how religion is viewed and practiced likely influences that too.

Growing up as Black Mormons, there was also a sense of being deviant from mainstream Mormonism because the latter wasn't necessarily meant to be for us. While I think my mom felt more comfortable in the mainstream for a long time, my siblings and I acknowledged and accepted our difference and made some efforts to distance ourselves from the expectation to assimilate in the ways older generations may have felt they needed to. My dad never joined the LDS Church, so he was already seen as deviant because he was a "non-member."

Ethnicity (and Race)

All of my family members are Black. We all have African ancestry, though, to different degrees. We have a range of skin tones, though we all tend to be on the lighter side except for my dad. Ethnicity is one thing; race is another thing. Ethnically, we are all of mixed heritage. We all have African and European ancestry. Some of us have South African ancestry, some have Northern European ancestry, and most of us have both Western European and West African ancestry. Ethnicity does not equal racial culture, especially considering how race has been weaponized as a way to denote class in many colonized areas.

In the US, my family is Black racially and culturally, though this is not usually the case in other places we have visited and lived. When I was in Brazil serving my LDS mission, I was seen as Black most of the time but notably of a "lighter" variety. Though I was living in Bahia—a notably Black and indigenous area—I was called a "Paulista" often, which refers to someone who lives in Sao Paulo. The deeper connotation here was that I had mixed African and European ancestry that matched mixed Black people in the wealthier, whiter southern states of Brazil. When my brother was in South Africa serving his LDS mission, he was seen as "coloured," a racial category that denotes mixed-race heritage.

In my interviews with family members, race was always mentioned over ethnicity. Most of my family members talked about experiences with race, since race is a social construct and therefore involves other people. The struggles of racial interactions were noticed by several family members. Reason and experience were often used to talk about race with my siblings. Some of my family members, like my dad, did not mention race at all. When it comes to intuition, I notice this is an acute ability for my siblings, much in the same way it is for my mom. Jette, James, and Morgan all talked clearly about how intuition and social cognition relate to how they navigate interactions with others, especially as Black people.

Socioeconomic Status

My family has gone through what a lot of Black families in the US go through—an evolution from poverty to a generally middle class standing. My parents were afforded some opportunities for education and work after civil rights legislation was put into effect to attempt some form of equity for African Americans. They both chose professions that would offer more financial security; my dad became a doctor, and my mom became a nurse.

In her interview, my mom talked about the impact of her poor, country upbringing and how she worked to change how she related to society once she was out of that setting. Both of my parents went into the military, which provided more opportunities to make money, see the world, and be of service to others. I know many African Americans who joined the military from older generations and saw the potential for upward mobility like my parents did. My parents eventually got to the point where they felt secure enough to have more children (Mom already had LaShawn), which is when all of my siblings came along.

My siblings and I have always identified as middle class from what I can remember. We don't talk about our social class nearly as much as we talk about other parts of our identity, as our interviews reflect. This doesn't mean we haven't had financial struggles, but they are not near what those in lower classes actually face continually.

For example, when we moved from North Carolina to Pennsylvania, my parents were financially responsible for two house notes until they could sell the North Carolina house. I was on a reduced lunch plan while in middle school because my family was considered low-income at the time. My dad's income was not enough to handle two house notes and then general family expenses. This lasted less than two years, and then I didn't qualify for that program anymore. My mom went back to work while I was in middle school and her income helped us live a more middle-class lifestyle. When we finally sold the North Carolina house, that really helped, and we were no longer considered low-income.

Now that we are all older, everyone still identifies as middle class. All of my siblings have bachelor's degrees, and by the time of this publication, all of us will likely have master's degrees. The determination to avoid poverty is alive and well within us, as we are acutely aware that we are always only a few unfortunate months away from poverty. Education is still seen as the best way to reduce the chances that this will be the case for us, though we are also aware that education can only do so much to combat the ills of prejudice and other external factors over which we have limited control. My nieces and nephew haven't expressed any financial insecurity or experienced it from my understanding.

Sexual Orientation

There has been an evolution in views on queerness in my family that closely matches larger societal acceptance of queer identity. Growing up in an LDS household, it was almost a given during my childhood that same-sex relationships were unacceptable. To be fair, I don't know that my siblings and I really thought about it until we were at least double digits in age. Morgan has the most vivid memories, it seems, about receiving messages about queer relationships at a young age. This is significant, as she would later date and then marry someone who identified as a woman. Morgan mentioned in her interview that she knows her queer identity is something she has to be aware of in more conservative spaces in order to feel safe, along with her other marginalized identities.

My parents seem to be open to queer relationships to some level, though my dad notably did not attend Morgan's wedding, and the rest of the family was upset about that. Arguably, my mom was the most vocal and passionate in her disagreement with him. My dad cited his Christian beliefs as the reason why he did not attend, and others in the family who also had Christian beliefs cited the reasons why Christ would be fine with our sister's gay marriage. This would have been a very different conversation a decade prior to Morgan's wedding, as more members of the family would have shared Dad's beliefs, though with more nuanced explanations. Fynn identifies as being gay, which has been embraced by my family. Fynn and Morgan have a special relationship around their queerness.

Indigenous Heritage

When I refer to indigenous heritage, I am speaking specifically about indigeneity to the land I am living on (the Americas). In my family, on both my parents' sides, there has always been an understanding that we have Indigenous American ancestry. Where my parents lived in South Carolina was home to the Cherokee people. However, a few of us have done ancestry tests, and no Native American ancestry shows up! It's likely that Fynn, Naiobi, and Nalani have Indigenous American ancestry, as they have Mexican heritage from their father's side. No one brought up indigenous heritage in their interviews, however.

National Origin

Everyone interviewed for this book was born and raised in the United States. We are all solely American citizens. LaShawn spent some of her childhood years in Germany with Mom, which may have had some impact on her perspective. We all identify as African American, with a specific American history of enslavement. We are descendants of enslaved Africans of the Transatlantic slave trade.

As American citizens, there is acknowledgement of the current privileges we enjoy by being free of the perils of war. We are able to watch others in incredible war crises and disengage whenever we want in ways that those in crisis cannot. At the same time, domestic terrorism is an increasing concern in the United States. Gun violence perpetrated by largely white American men puts lives at stake daily, while other countries look on in confusion and concern as it shifts some of their ideas of the American Dream. As an African American family, becoming targets of radicalized violence is a concern we talk about openly. As many of my family members discussed navigating social situations in their interviews, increasing feelings of safety and decreasing threats to safety is important because of the social climate we live in as African American citizens.

Gender

We are a female-heavy family. I interviewed 7 females and 3 males for this book. This reflects a lot of how I experienced family life growing up. Interestingly, while there was more female than male representation, there were patriarchal elements to how the family ran. My parents, because they were raised Christian in the South during a time when the Black family was in a phase of restructuring, viewed men as the head of the home. As such, they were seen as providers and protectors. They were meant to be decision-makers. This trickled into the home my siblings and I were raised in. I don't recall this ever being an explicit statement in my home, but we learned at church about this divine structure of the home. I learned that I was meant to be a nurturer and mother to my children. I learned that I was supposed to yield to my husband as he yields to the Lord once I was married. It wasn't until I was an adult that I asked my dad about leadership in the family, and he told me that he believed men should be the leaders of the home. For some reason, I was shocked to hear him say that.

As an adult, I also learned about the idea that in Black families, boys are loved by their parents, while girls are raised. This is about differences in displays of affection and emotional connection between parents and children. There are many Black folks I've spoken to who have had this experience. They watched the boys in their families grow up being admired, adored, and generally not held accountable for irresponsible or inappropriate behavior. Girls, on the other hand, were expected to follow rules, take care of others, and take responsibility for people, places, and things that really were not appropriate. I did not notice this disparity in treatment in my family, but other siblings did. James also acknowledges that this was likely true, as he did not internalize childhood experiences as being harmful as much as the rest of us did.

My dad and I at my PhD commencement ceremony

Dr. James Curtiss Jones is a retired, respected cardiothoracic surgeon. He was in practice for 30+ years. He is the father of our family. Over his lifetime, he has traveled all over the world for mountain climbing, hiking, and other outdoor activities. He currently spends most of his time in Southern California, where he and my mom share a home.

14

DAD

This chapter is a transcript of my full interview with my father, James Curtiss Jones.

~

Niecie: Dad, what does it mean to know something?

Dad: I'm aware that there are diverse viewpoints on what it means to know something. However, my own viewpoint is that knowing something is believing that there is overwhelming evidence that it is true.

Niecie: What are some core beliefs that you feel like you know?

Dad: I'm going to give you some of these right now. Two of my core beliefs are as follows. Number one, no person is better than another person. Number two, God is sovereign in the affairs of the world.

Niecie: And how did you come to know these?

Dad: I have arrived at these beliefs through Bible study, experience, and reason.

Niecie: How has your family influenced what you know?

Dad: My parents influenced what I know by encouraging me to study the Bible.

Niecie: What has your family taught you that you believe to be true?

Dad: My parents told me to live by the golden rule; that is, that I should treat other people as I myself would wish to be treated. That is one of the most important things that they told me.

Niecie: Let's talk about the different ways of knowing that I'll be talking about in my book. You talked about some of these already, but what would you say you know by way of authority?

Dad: I know by way of authority, reason, experience and intuition that God is sovereign in the affairs of the world.

Niecie: What do you know by way of social cognition?

Dad: I know the following. Number one, people sometimes behave unkindly to their contemporaries. Number two, people can forsake their unkind behaviors and become kind, considerate individuals.

Niecie: What ways of knowing do you find yourself leaning on more than the others, if any?

Dad: I probably lean on authority more than any other way of knowing.

Niecie: What knowledge have you tried to pass on to your family?

Dad: I have tried to pass on to my family that it is best to live by biblical principles. I have done this more by example than by precept.

Niecie: Moving on to the flow state questions, how would you say you experience the flow state?

Dad: One of the main ways I experience the flow state is by listening to music, especially classical music and jazz. All I require to attain this state is to sit quietly and relax. Here are some other ways I experience the flow state. Number one, reading uplifting literature in English or German. Number two, camping and hiking in the wilderness. Number three, walking or jogging along the seashore.

Mom receiving a prestigious academic award

Dr. Dianne McAdams-Jones is a professor of nursing and practitioner of equity, diversity, and inclusion at Utah Valley University. She is the recipient of the 2022 Black Academic Excellence Award for being the first Black professor to receive full professorship at Utah Valley University. She is also the matriarch of our family. She enjoys spending time with family and friends and traveling. She splits her time between Southern California and Utah.

15

MOM

*This chapter includes excerpts from my interview with my
mother, Dianne McAdams-Jones.*

∼

On What She Knows for Sure

I know I have to plan my future. I know I have to be aware of where I'm going to land before I jump. I know that I have to plan for me. I know that nobody cares more about me than me. I've learned that over time, and I know that I have to surround myself with people who care as much about me as I care about them. We have to understand enough about each other that we can manage a space among ourselves. I found that people with whom I have shared space growing up and in college have been my better connections. We share some of the same values, and we know some of the same things. [I know] that we have to know who we are and who's going to plan for us.

[In the past] I watched my surroundings, and I watched

what my purpose was in the spaces that I was in. My purpose was to fuel other people's lives. Along the way, I was fortunate because [by] watching other people; I saw bits and pieces of myself. I saw how their lives were shaping, and I figured I better be aware of all of my surroundings so I could see how mine was shaping so I wouldn't arrive at some of the spaces where they were arriving.

I think being a nurse helped me understand a lot about people and a lot about myself. I saw that in a lot of spaces — some of the paths I had chosen — to be a mom and to be a wife put me in a caretaker mode, which was fine. I don't mind being in a caretaker mode.

But I also realized that caring for everybody else does not mean forgetting to care about yourself. Don't expect people you care for to look after you. I'm still responsible for me is what I learned. Some marriages and families turn out where there's one person that's a total nurturer and a care-taker. I realized that was a role I assumed, and I assumed it because I wanted to assume it, which is why I managed it, I think, very well. It wasn't a cumbersome thing for me, but I also realized that there was an end to the nurturing and fueling other people's lives. Then I had to infuse myself with life and I had to do something for myself.

If I could say one thing about being in the "hood," parenthood—each child is different, and parents don't get any instructions for any one child. You manage each child as best you can and, more often than not, we manage them with blanket orders, [like] "No watching TV," "Be quiet!" or "No, everybody go to bed." Either way, we usually get told later that we mismanaged everything. You aren't going to get it all right. There are so many things I wished I had done or could have done, but that ship has sailed. There is no going back. It's done. I must suffer the consequences.

What I have learned is this—I must forgive myself. I must accept what "tongue lashings" I get from my children. Yes, there have been "tongue lashings." I accept them all. I have learned not to push back even if I don't remember anything they are illuminating from the past. If they remember it, that is all that matters. It is real to them, thus, it is fact. [I have to] keep my opinions to myself. I will just accept it. If allowed, I apologize. That is all I can do, plus remember to not repeat the offenses.

Then, my mental and physical health. I work very hard on eating healthy, exercising, and thinking positively while noticing the negativity with a pure and immense desire to avoid it. I am a spiritual person and I work hard on doing the right thing, the thing that keeps me out of harm's way while not harming others. [That] and keeping my opinions to myself.

On Family Influence

My dad was an orderly, and that's like a nursing assistant. He was a male nursing assistant, and he wanted me to be a registered nurse. The registered nurses had told him what to do and had caught him sleeping, [and they] had written him up. [He told me,] "Oh yeah, you be a registered nurse." And by default, I took that on.

See, that's another thing. Parents said things to you when we were growing up. That was the bomb. That was what you did. You didn't question it. I thought, "Yeah, if that's what he wants me to be, that's what my daddy said." I liked what he did, and I just [thought it was] cool that he would come take our temperatures when we were sick. That was a big deal. I developed somewhere in my brain a liking for healthcare, and I became a nurse. We listened. Some of us did. So that was not a foreign thought or idea for me to listen to my parents.

My parents were not educated. They had no idea [about post-secondary education]. I was off their payroll in college. The expectation was you go to college, you get an education, you do well, and you come back and help at home. That is how that worked. There was nobody standing over there looking to see if you were making the right step or not. They expected you to work, make the right step. That just was the expectation, and it was the expectation of all of my colleagues, my classmates. We all had the same expectations from our parents.

I don't live in my children's lives. I may have thought one day that I would, but I'm appreciative of that because, see, that's what you want to see. Your children grow up and get out, and you just be available if they ask you for some advice. But if they don't really need your advice, you can just keep it to yourself. That's just the way life is. It isn't the same way it was when I was growing up, and that's okay. What life does, it's evolutionary. It changes, and it changes because environments change.

On Authority

In every space I've been in, there have been authoritative figures, and it isn't so much that I look at them and say, "I'm going to be that." Some of it—50% of it—is that. I don't begrudge them for who they are. I looked at them in a time when I believed, "This is what you're given."

I had teachers that I thought did great things. They were lovely people, and I felt warm around them. I wanted to be some of the things that they were. That was in school—in elementary school—with African American teachers.

In high school, [I experienced this] with non-melanated —the traditional "white"—people. Same thing. I saw things in them that I thought that'd be nice.

I went to Tuskegee,[1] all Black people mostly. I saw people there and thought, "Oh, that's so great to see that, to be that." And I was also growing in myself at the time and having the lumps and bumps that you have when you grow as a teenager. I was only 16 to 20, so I [was] still a teenager— total country bumpkin—getting out of the country with no running water straight from the cotton fields. Now, I'm in a city around fairly well-to-do Black people, and I'm seeing things with them that I think is great.

On Intuition, Experience, Reason, and Social Cognition

Intuition—that's a good thing, but it has to be honed. You can intuitively think you got it, and you miss it. You missed the mark because what you thought wasn't what it really was. [Intuition is] being aware of my surroundings and listening, but not necessarily taking action until I am sure of the intuition that I think I'm getting or the vibes I think I'm getting. I am cautious.

I have made a lot of mistakes intuitively with people, thinking that they were my friends and they weren't. That has called me into thinking about my thinking about people and to draw the conclusion that I'm interested in people that are interested in me. We have similar behaviors, [which] makes the relationship a lot easier. I don't question so much, but I don't openly pick up people for friends anymore because of that very thing.

---

1. My mom is referring to Tuskegee University, which was called Tuskegee Institute when she attended.

Cognitively learning from people and having lived experiences—that builds your intuition. Intuition is grounded in a sense of something in yourself. It's DNA, 97% of it. You can't control the two eyes, the two eyebrows, the hair, the nose, the nostrils, the mouth, the ears. 97% of all of us are the same. It's that other 3% that you develop epigenetically. And that's that lived experience—the things you learn, the senses you get about something.

Critical thinking would be essential in the world of healthcare. My lived experiences—which are not given to me—they're lived, and I experience them every day in order for me to have intuition. You learn how to critically think [after learning a skill] because there is no real algorithm that explains and tells you everything to do for every patient that you see. There's probably a basic template about some treatment for different behaviors, but a lot of your intuition and lived experience when handling these kinds of cases help you to decide sometimes which path to take. Sometimes you make a path [because] there is no path to take. That's critical thinking for me as a nurse because everything isn't written out on paper for me to do when I go in for a patient.

That's just reading tea leaves. What that really is is just reading your surroundings—being cognizant of where you are, where you're situated, what's around you. Yeah, that's one of the biggest ones. I'd say 75% of it is that. And then the rest of it just sort of falls in place. Sometimes I'm wrong about some "tea leaves" I've read, but I am careful not to act now. That's what intuition tells me: don't act until you are absolutely sure. If you can wait, let somebody else make another move. The more moves people make, the better. I can read the tea leaves, but I think 75% of that knowing is that gut feeling—generated, likely, from an accumulation of experiences.

On Flow

I haven't always been in it. We came from Pennsylvania to [Utah], and I popped into the clinical setting at the county hospital. For some reason, I managed very well there. I got a good flow [with] people that could laugh and talk and work together. It was good because we depended on each other to save the patient. Nobody was losing a patient or having a problem on our shift. We worked together. That's a concept that I don't think happens a lot of times in clinical nursing. When I read what my students tell me, I don't think a lot of them feel like they're in a flow, which is why they leave the profession. I hit that place, and I was in the flow.

When I got to the academic setting, that was harder because of a lot of things. I had come from a world where I had been in charge in the military. It didn't matter whether you had melanin or not; your rank gave you the chain of command. I arrived in a different space when I was in the clinical setting. I knew my role. We had charge nurses, and no, I was not a charge nurse. I was only [working] part-time, and that was fine that I wasn't. I knew what the goal was among all of us. It was to keep our patients alive, don't make any mistakes, and watch out for each other. If you see something, say something. That's always the case. That was the flow. I didn't have to figure that flow out.

[In] academia, I had to figure that flow out—a whole lot more things going on there. Feeling in the flow is one thing. Feeling out of the flow is another thing. I had the most problems when I was out of the flow because I couldn't read people. I was going through that at the hospital plus working in the academic setting.

You [kids] were big enough to get a hot dog [by that point.] You were going to school and stuff, but emotionally I wasn't there for you because all my emotions I think were taken up between those two jobs. Being in nursing, I can't make mistakes. It took all of my critical thinking skills, all of my emotions. Everything had to be focused and fine-tuned. I'm taking care of patients; it's patients' lives. Thankfully, I didn't harm anyone, and that's in my past. I wasn't in the flow of things with my kids because I was disconnected. I came home, and all I thought about was what happened at work.

[I have] a good flow now because I go to work when I have to be there for a meeting. I don't teach any face-to-face classes. I don't have to go every day. If I want to sleep in, I can sleep in. If I have a meeting at 9 [am] or 10 [am,] technically speaking, I could be in my jammies. Usually, I'm not, because if I'm in my jammies, I feel jammy. I always have to brush my teeth, wash my face. If I didn't take a shower the night before, I'm going to take a shower. I'm going to be ready from head to toe when I sit before that camera for a meeting.

I think employers have seen that sometimes it's just as effective, if not more, when people work from home. In academia, it's kind of been this way a bit anyway, with the online education meetings. The flow is pretty good. As a matter of fact, I look forward to going in to work because there's a break for me. I get to see people, and I am a people person.

I can't say that I have a complaint at all about the flow now. It's a pretty good rhythm, but I have no little children to be responsible for. Everybody around me is grown. I have access to children when I want access, and when I don't want access, I don't have to have access. I can take naps when I want. I can get up and go somewhere. I can read, I can go shopping, I can go to my doctor appointments. It's a great flow. There are a lot less moving parts. I only have to worry about the constructs that affect me. It's a good flow.

This is why I'm not really ready to retire, because I like to have something to do. I tell people at work, "Who am I going to blame my problems on if I quit work?" I like to have a purpose. I think self-actualization, which is the top rung on Maslow's hierarchy of needs, is a place where we all would like to be, where we self-actualize and we feel like we have control of things. Right now, I have control of a lot of things, and that's a good feeling.

LaShawn behind the scenes of a media appearance

Dr. LaShawn Williams is the owner of her therapy and coaching private practice, Relational Spaces. She is also an assistant professor with 20 years' experience in higher education. She is a sought-after speaker and presenter for her range of knowledge and experience. She is the mother of Fynn, Naiobi, and Nalani.

16

LASHAWN

This chapter includes excerpts from my interview with my sister, LaShawn Williams.

〜

On What Knowing Is

To know something...it's like on a continuum of understanding something, but then also being able to embody it. Knowing something is thinking, feeling, and doing. It's like the connection of all things. Something in your mind—you experience some sort of emotion—and that then connects with what you know. Then your body actually has to do what you know. Knowing how to ride a bike is different from knowing how to trust people, but it's still kind of a similar process. What you experience and then what you embody to me is how you know something.

On What She Knows for Sure

That, for me, depends on what dimension of life I'm in. What I knew at 8 is different from what I knew at 18, at 28, 38. Right now, things that I feel like I know to be true? For myself, I feel like I know joy as a deep undercurrent in my life, despite everything happening at the surface. Externally, I know joy in an undeniable way because even in my lowest of time periods, I have known this electrical undercurrent in my life that just sits there. That says there is still joy here, and I just know it. I just know joy. There's this feeling of deep contentment, and it is this undercurrent in my life.

For me, it's this undercurrent that's always there, always present. I can't say that I have always known it. Even in the depths of understanding depression or a depressive episode —I still could feel even if I couldn't access joy. I knew that it was there, and, inclusive of everything else, that was still there. It didn't need me to be joyful, but it was just there. I know joy as a deep, fulfilling undercurrent in my life. I know that to be true.

Other things that I feel like I know are the ability to detach myself from sources of suffering. That took a while to learn that. Lots of disappointment in relationships and human connections.

Also, once I knew that I didn't have to believe everything my mind told me, I had a lot more permission to not take things personally. I specifically remember I was reading *The Mastery of Love* by Don Miguel Ruiz, and he was talking about when you are in a relationship, and you're in a bad mood, you want your partner to come take care of you or whatever. Your partner's like, "Hey, you know what? You're in a bad mood. I'm going to go play and when you feel better, come hang out, come let me know. I want to hang out and play with you."

I remember at that time of life, I was like, "Why would they do that? It's so rude. It's so inconsiderate. How could you not care about your partner being in pain?" Hello, codependency. But knowing now that's very legit, to believe that somebody is a whole human being, and that they can take care of themselves. You don't have to be attached to why they're upset or why they're suffering, especially if you didn't cause it.

I know now that I don't have to internalize or metabolize every experience of suffering that I have. I can detach from it, I can observe it, I can have a response to it, but I don't have to actually embody that. I know that's a truth for me, that I can remove myself from sources of suffering in a pretty concrete way.

I've always loved reading self-help books. I've always loved reading relationship books. I would read a lot of books trying to understand the relationship that I was in, trying to understand the marriage and all of those things. I love books. Books are a big way of how I come to know things because I truly believe I can't be the only person that's gone through whatever I'm going through. Somebody has to have written a book about it somewhere. I don't want to be the one to write the book. I know if I can find a book of somebody else's words, words helped me know things.

On Family Influence

My most consistent field of learning is my family system, especially because we moved around a lot [when I was younger]. I feel like my family is legit where I learned another piece for me, which is, there's a difference between the role and the person. My mother is the role; Dianne is the person. When I learned to differentiate between the expectations I had of my mom, I learned to understand Dianne in a certain kind of way. Same thing with my dad. There was my dad, and there was Carold. There was my [step]dad, and there was Jim Jones.

I learned from my family quickly [that] my parents were people. The expectations that I had of my parents, I needed to figure out what are those expectations compared to what the person is actually able to do and who that person actually is. Then, how can I detach myself from the expectations I have about what this role that they have is supposed to do in my life? Who they're supposed to be because they're my mom, my dad, or whatever?

Learning that role was different from that person. That's what my family, particularly my parents, taught me. Even though I couldn't say, "Oh, I'm going to have a relationship with Dianne, the person" when I differentiated my mother from Dianne, my dad from Carold, my stepdad from Jim Jones, it helped me be able to kind of manage my expectations, pace some of my energies. I don't know that I could necessarily articulate it as a kid, but as a young adult, especially differentiating and coming out of some really very deep enmeshment patterns, I had to realize what was I separating from because there was mom stuff, and then there was Dianne stuff, and there was dad stuff.

I feel like I learned stuff to be true [from my family], but maybe not stuff that I would necessarily, I don't know, agree with. I guess I feel like I learned to do things. I learned to be independent. I learned to be a caretaker. I learned to do things. I learned to perform roles. That's what I learned.

So far as my family teaching me any sort of life truths, I don't resonate with that so much. I guess I wish that I could, or I feel like I'm supposed to, but I know that my family taught me how to perform roles. When I think about family, I don't think about myself and my siblings. I think about my parents, what my parents taught me. What my parents taught me was I am supposed to perform specific roles. I am supposed to bridge gaps. I'm supposed to anticipate needs. I learned to adjust to situations. What I experienced and what I learned to be true I feel like are two very different things. I know that's a lot of what I experienced.

On Authority

I don't value learning at all by somebody in power. I've always been, I guess, rebellious, or I've always questioned things. That was easier to do outside of the home than inside. Some things I learned by authority were things like having confidence in myself. I think about Chief Master Sergeant Cecil F. McLaurin. He was my teacher in Junior ROTC. Few people, I think, have been able to have authority or influence in my life like he did.

I remember it. I was [in high school] walking across the courtyard going home, and we were walking past each other. He comes up to me and says, "What classes are you taking next year for your electives?" I was like, "I'm typing." I was going to take typing and something else. He's like, "I want you to come do ROTC." And for whatever reason, I had never thought about doing ROTC, but I went, and I signed up for it.

The first day of class, Chief put me in the front of the class and made me the flight commander. I know I looked scared because I'm a very shy person. E. E. Smith was [where I attended] high school. I started there in 10th grade. This was my senior year. I'm super quiet. I don't talk to people. I'm very, very shy. It was an all Black high school. I was coming into my Blackness in different ways. I'd never been in an all Black environment before, but it was one of the best environments in my whole life. I love my high school experience.

Chief said, "Take ROTC," and I was like, "Okay, cool." So, I took ROTC, and I was the flight commander for the first day of class. I remember hearing everybody murmuring, "Ooh, she's so scared, she's so nervous. Look at her. Oh my god, she's about to cry." But I gained people's respect being placed in that position of authority. What I learned by way of authority, by listening to Chief, I gained confidence in myself.

I also credit my mom. She's one of the people that I think also taught me confidence in a different way. I always give the example with her when I had to give a talk [in church] on Easter Sunday and she had me stand up in the middle of the living room all night. I had to practice my Primary[1] talk until 2 or 3 am to make sure I had the inflections, the tone, everything about how Jesus said Mary's name when he was resurrected. My mother [said], "Again. Again." I had to go through my talk over and over and over again. My mother's authority and Chief's authority are the two major examples of what I've learned about myself through authority.

On Reason

Reason for me is critical thinking. I feel like that's been one of the major things that I've had to use to survive. I thor-

---

1.   Primary is the LDS church program for children 18 months old to 11 years old.

oughly believe that there has to be a reason for everything. Some stuff I'm like, "There ain't no way. This doesn't make any sense. Why is this sort of a thing happening?"

For me, reason is all about—it's, one, surviving. Once you survive something, then you try to make sense of it. Things that I've learned or that I know to be true by way of reasoning—I study relationships. I study people. I try and understand why people do things that they do or [why] they don't do things that they should do.

Knowing things by reasoning through them and by thinking through them, I do trust myself to be able to figure something out. I feel like I can think about something to the point where I can let other stuff go, but I refuse to not think my way through something.

There's got to be a process. There's got to be a pattern. That's one of the things that Harriet Lerner—in one of her books—she says, "Pay attention to patterns, not people." That was another way that I was able to differentiate the parent and the person—pay attention to the pattern.

What's the parenting pattern? What's the discipline pattern? What's the relationship pattern that you have with this parent? Then who was the person? If those two things are different, which they normally are, I had to reason my way into understanding my expectations for my parents and my expectations and the realities of the people. There were going to be limitations about what my parents could do because of the people that they were.

I didn't serve a mission for my church. I'm not going to go and lie for y'all [the LDS Church].

"Why did the priesthood ban happen?"

"Because they were racist." There's not going to be anything around me that allows me to give an answer besides what the truth is. I reasoned that because I couldn't fit into what I was supposed to actually say socially, what I was supposed to think about being a member of this church, and this faith, and its racism. I reasoned myself out of going on a mission. I was like, "I'm not going to do that."

If something doesn't make sense, I can't go with it. I need something to make sense, at least in my mind. If I can make sense of it, I can deal with it, I can tolerate it, I can make space for it, I can accept it, and I can engage it in some way. It's got to make sense.

I think I'm logical, and I reason probably to a detrimental toxic fault in some ways. I thoroughly believe in the ability to know things by reasoning through it and studying and looking at things. I love religions, too. I love mysticism and how it teaches us to simply be. I feel like I've always loved the cool stuff. Reading in religions about the mysteries of the kingdom and then with Christianity, I'm like, "How come no one was talking about the mysteries of the kingdom? What does that mean?" You give me some books on mysticism, and I am all the way in because I believe in the beauty of the mind to make sense of things.

On Experience

By way of experience, I know how to get through things. I know how to survive, and I know how to not ask for help. I know how to be independent. Those have been my major experiences—knowing that I can get through just about anything and knowing what I can't get through.

Also, through experience, I have learned that my most reliable assumption is to assume I have to figure [things] out and that no one's coming to rescue me. Through experience, that's one of the many things that I've learned. No one's coming to rescue me. That's why I value reason. I figure I can figure it out. There's got to be a way. I have learned that through experience.

That's where I've learned that undercurrent of joy—through experience—and being able to recognize, "Yep, things are awful. Things are really hard. Things are super difficult." Based on what I'm in right now, my perspective, my experience, relatively speaking, there's stuff people go through. I'm like, "I couldn't do it. I wouldn't, couldn't do it." For the things that I have experienced, I've learned survival. I don't know if it's a healthy or unhealthy independence, but I've learned to figure it out. I've learned to not ask questions, and I've learned to go to things that I feel like are pretty unchangeable.

That's probably why I read a lot of books. I feel like books are unchangeable or less changeable than people. I think people are fickle. So, for me, I will look to a book for an answer before I look to a person. That's been something that I think I've learned through experience.

On Intuition

It was you that told me a couple years ago to trust my intuition, and I didn't know what that meant. I committed myself to being open to trying to understand what that might mean. Getting into and out of mysticism, these different phases and different people have brought different experiences into my life. Tarot cards, oracle cards, and things like that. What experiences like oracle cards and tarot cards taught me was confirmation of what you said to me, to trust my own intuition.

I did not know that what I experienced for many, many years—decades—of my life was intuition. I don't know which "voyant" it is—clairvoyant, audio, cognitive—I don't know which "voyant" it is, but I have had intuition ever since I was at least a teenager. I don't think I'm clairvoyant where I can necessarily see things, but I've *seen* things. I'm not [clairaudient] where I hear things, but I've *heard* things. I've asked a question to a person, and they've told me something, and I've known that's not the answer. I have known, for whatever reason I've known it, the answer is actually this. But you're not going to ever get that answer from this question, this relationship, or this person.

Listening to you and believing that maybe there is something to this idea of intuition and trying to figure out what it is, the clarity that's come with intuition. With allowing it to just show up, and for me to know that's what that is. That's what that's been this whole time and every single time. Getting to the point where I can actually start to predict it at times.

It's so frustrating. There are so many things that I know through intuition. I'm like, "Damn, I can't say anything about this? I just get to know it?" I get so upset. I'm like, "I just get to know this and not say anything about it?" I have learned, through intuition, there are things that I'm going to know that I can't say a thing about. I just have to know that there are things that I know that are going to help me out in the future situation. I just have to wait until it comes to pass. There are things that I'm going to know about that are going to lead me to ask a different question or another question or to do a thing or to not do a thing. My intuition, the more that I develop it and the more that I commit to tapping into it, it's cool. It's really interesting, but it's also just really weird.

For my work as a therapist, I'll meet a client, and I'll know what direction we're heading in. They'll say something, and I'm like, "Okay, this is going to connect to this because this is probably a thing that's happening." I don't think that's therapeutic [training]. I think it's intuition because it's different with every single client, and it doesn't fit in with what I was taught in school. I know the difference between assumptions and intuition, and that, to me, is significant.

What do I know [just] by intuition? I feel like I know how to trust myself in interactions with others because, [through] my intuition, I either see a scene, I hear a conversation, I hear an answer. I think when it's loud enough, I have dreams. When I have those dreams and those intuitions, I just know to make room for them. I know to accept them. I know not to question them.

On Social Cognition

A book that gave this to me and informs how I show up in these interpersonal ways was *Siddhartha* by Hermann Hesse. There's a scene when Siddhartha is crossing the river, and the riverboat conductor or driver—he says something about the complete circle of life and that there is value in people no matter their positioning. There's value in someone who robs, and there's value in someone who gives.

There's a certain phrase that he tells Siddhartha that allows Siddhartha to kind of have this whole metacognitive, inclusive, spiritual experience about good and evil being necessary, like yin and yang. There's a little yin in yang. There's light in every bit of dark and dark and every bit of light.

I think studying therapy prepared me to be a parent in ways that I wasn't prepared ever before. I just knew that there were things I did not want to do as a parent, and then I had to let my kids teach me how to parent them. I have learned mostly about this through parenting my kids. I remember having to tell myself in very specific terms, "I should reach out and pick up my child and hold them. I should cuddle them."

There wasn't anything in me that naturally thought to do that. I remember having to tell myself, "You need to reach out," and I needed to comfort my child or hold their hand or pick them up and hug them. I needed to touch my child. I remember having to tell myself to do that because of books I read, number one, but also because of learning with my kids what they needed as little humans.

Growing up, kids were just these things that I took care of. [I was the] oldest of five, [and there was an] eight year difference between me and my siblings. All my siblings, to me, were people to take care of. They weren't people. They weren't, like, connections to me. Yeah, little siblings and whatnot, but I take care of them.

Carrying that into becoming a parent, knowing that I want to have a relationship with my kids, this is more than someone to take care of. This is someone to have a relationship with. When it's your kids and you're trying to do the best you can, my training as a therapist is what taught me to slow down and to allow myself to think reasonably. "What is it that I need to do in this situation?" I believe that I am a nurturing person. I believe that I am a caring person, but I know that there were things I had to teach myself to do.

For me, a big thing was learning how to manage men's attractions to me. I had to be aware of how people looked at me and watched me. I had some really negative experiences as a kid, too, that I think impacted me figuring out connection with men and just with people in general. There are some things I feel like I didn't learn so far as social cognition. There were some times where I just did not pick up on social cues.

I still don't pick up on social cues. I'm like, "Other people just know this. They understand that when that thing was said, they're supposed to have a certain reaction to it." I didn't realize I didn't pick up on social cues. I can think back to my teens, and part of it I blame on moving around so much and always being a new kid and always being quiet. You don't get a chance to really interact with a lot of people.

People never talked to me in public, and I didn't understand what that was. But that's one of the things that led me to be a therapist. I realized I was a really good listener. People would speak to me, and they would share things with me. I meet people in public places, and somehow or another, within five minutes, I've learned their life story. I didn't ask, but people, they just tell me things.

I learned something about how to be safe for people in a social cognition [way]. I learned how to be safe. I learned how to hold space. I think I learned how to be quiet. A lot of being quiet was about surviving and not being bullied. Something, also, about me learning to be quiet, I think, told people that there was something sincere and genuine about me, that they could trust me with their secrets. Maybe that's the interpersonal piece. I learned to hold people's secrets and to recognize that there was something about me that made them feel comfortable enough to tell me their secrets. I knew that I was supposed to keep them.

Going back to intuition, there's a lot of things that I would see or know that I knew I couldn't say anything about. I was just supposed to witness them. I think things that I've learned through social cognition that I understand now is the power of witnessing people, seeing them, seeing their stories, and allowing their stories to be true. That's their story. That's their experience.

On Flow

The way that I think about flow is not zoning out but this idea about being present. I have noticed it when it's happening. I've experienced it in the classroom, when I've had a really powerful guest speaker, and we're just all enraptured in the moment. I had a hospice social worker that came and talked to my class, and I experienced flow. When you can feel it in the room—not like tension so thick you can cut it with a knife—but you feel what's in the room while that person is speaking and sharing their story. To me, that's flow. We were in that story with her as she was talking about people choosing to release and choosing to leave. It's what gives me a deep respect for death doula work that people are doing because I think you have to be in flow. You have to be in what's there when that's happening.

For me to get into flow, it's an interesting question. I know, when I drop into myself, I associate it with being able to be productive, but I also get into flow. I love business ideas. I love the idea of being an entrepreneur. I love the idea of creativity, and sharing thoughts, and being able to put things together in a way that I think is accessible.

I love challenging myself to make more accessible language in how I speak or share about principles or insights that I have. I will find myself very easily in flow when I'm creating something. I think for some people—"Oh my gosh, business development? Entrepreneur?"—it can be so exhausting. For me, it's reciprocal. I get so much out of just being creative in that sense. That, to me, is a place where I get to be creative, when I'm thinking about building my business.

I'm also someone where if you just put me on the stage to do something, I guess I get into flow there, and I can do it.

If I don't need a lot of prep time, I just need to be in the place. Even if I've prepared words to speak, I usually don't use them because whatever is in that moment is what I tap into, and that's what I say. I've done it in all of my public speaking.

Whenever I'm asked to give a talk at church, or I'm asked to speak, [or] do a keynote, I try so hard to stick to what I've written down. Without fail, I can't do it. I tap into whatever is there, and I say what I think needs to be said. I can tell when it doesn't land. It doesn't mean that I'm not in flow. I'm saying that I don't like it because I'm in my head, and I don't feel like it lands, and I want to go back and redo it. I can consciously move myself into flow, but I can also just be in touch with whatever it is and show up.

However, I've not been comfortable being inside my own body for whatever those things are for me. That is why I pursued yoga training. I've done a 200-hour yoga training. I've done a 300-hour yoga training because of the somatics. I wanted to be able to sit. I realized that I felt like I couldn't sit with people.

I mean, I could do it on accident. I could sit with people, but I felt like I could only sit with them up to a point. I wanted to be able to sit with people, and I realized I can't sit with myself. So, in order for me to be able to sit with myself, how can I go and train? I was like, "I will go do yoga because it will allow me to sit with myself and sit with my body, connect with my body, learn all these different things." I love learning.

I love music. There are certain songs that I can put on, and they take me other places. I deeply love music. I love the intricacies of sound. And that's funky because I have severe hearing loss in one of my ears. That might be why I love music so much as I do, because I love being able to hear all the things. Music is just magic for me, and the right song—it puts me where I need to be. That's an activity puts me in a flow state.

Business ideas put me in flow state. Some quiet and solitude puts me in flow state. I'm not a big meditator, but I do love being mindful. I love being able to tap into the transcendent or the observant parts of me. The part of me that's sitting and the part of me that notices that my body is sitting on a couch. I love tapping into that. That helps me get into a flow state. Sometimes it's quiet and solitude, but other times it's music.

I love water. Water is a cool thing. I love sand. Water is a fun thing for me. I love the sound of the aquarium, like the water that's in there. I like being able to hear that sound. I've always liked little water fountains. I've liked the sounds of running water. I've always liked sand. Sand puts me in a flow state. Being at the beach, oh my gosh, and walking on the sand. Walking in the water just where the waves meet the beach, and where you sink. That's just otherworldly for me. The beach at night puts me in that sort of a flow state because the stars and the water are the same thing, and it just reflects.

On Passing Things on to Family

I think a lot of the things that I pass on to my kids is a lot of what I've learned about. People are different from the roles. Quickly teaching my kids that, "Hey, before I do all this mommy stuff, you're dealing with LaShawn. LaShawn is trying to do this mom stuff, and I may not be great at it, but I need you to know that it's your mom isn't failing you. It's LaShawn." That's learning what it means to be a mom.

Teaching my kids to have relationships with each other

where they trust each other, they believe each other, they look out for each other. Yes, they take care of each other, but it's not just that they take care of each other. I don't want them seeing each other as "My brother and my sister, I take care of them." I want them to say, "Hey, that's my best friend. That's my brother. I love that person." I need them to be the first people to call them out, but the first people to defend them. For me, passing that on to my kids, making sure that they know that I want them to be a team. Together—me and the kids—we are a team, and we are people doing this thing called life together.

I don't like sibling rivalry. I don't think, "Oh, we're siblings. We fight all the time." I don't like that. No, you're human beings. You don't treat people like that. My kids [have] helped me be a little more tolerant of things, but I'm like, "I need to know that you don't really think that way about your sibling. I don't want that kind of energy with you."

I just try and pass on to my kids that we are a team. We love each other because we hold each other accountable, and we love each other because we defend each other. We don't let anybody hurt our family, and we don't hurt our family. That's the thing that I've tried to make sure I pass on to my kids and teach them and also experience and embody with them.

James and his advisor, Dr. Cornel West, on his graduation day

James Curtiss Jones II is a theological justice, equity, and inclusion consultant. He is a two-time graduate of Union Theological Society in New York City. He is a prominent advocate for marginalized voices in Mormonism via his podcast, *Beyond the Block*. James is also a voice over artist, choreographer, and musician with a variety of projects he has worked on over the years.

17

JAMES

This chapter includes excerpts from my interview with my brother, James Curtiss Jones II.

~

On What He Knows for Sure

I know that I'm loved. I know that humans are not quite alone on this planet and that there's something beyond us, powers beyond us that we don't understand. I know that racism definitely exists. This is an indisputable fact to me. What else do I know? I know I exist. I know my existence matters.

My experiences taught that to me growing up [that racism exists]. Then I discovered that there were people that studied this kind of thing for a living. People had been keeping statistics, keeping records, keeping histories. You could say I came to it through both lived experience—I guess what you would call an epistemological learning—but also a rational learning. As in, I can see and observe statistically how Black people are treated in this country. I can reason that because of how disparately we are treated in this country that racism is a reality. So, it's a combination of both lived experience, that observation there, and also the observation of the data that exists outside of me, as well.

On Family Influence

I wasn't told most things to believe in terms of what I know. I mean, when you're a child, your parents tell you how to move, how to operate, even what to believe to an extent. But more often than not, your family shows you more than tells you what to know. I would say that how my family has influenced what I know has been demonstrated and shown more than told. That I'm loved is one of those things. That how we treat people matters. That there's a big difference between what we say we believe and what we believe. That was a big one.

I definitely learned the existence of the Divine more strongly through family. I've learned that I know my childhood still affects me to this day. A big part of who I am is a direct result of what has happened in my home and in my interactions with family. I know that how I've shown up in various relationships in my life is a result of what has happened or what I was shown in my family dynamic.

As terrible as this sounds, I learned that people have feelings. I know that people are people and deserve to be treated as human. I learned that in my family, again, shown more than told. I think my first encounters of other people's emotions occurred in the home. [It was my] first encounter with understanding that people, other people besides myself, matter. That definitely occurred in the home.

One thing I feel like I've learned more from my family

than I'm able to articulate is simply how I show up in the world and how people remark that I show up in the world. I feel like a lot of Black men, in particular, have had family situations similar to mine—where the mother has kind of doted on them, and treated them better than their sisters, and gave them really problematic ideas of how they can interact with women in the world.

For whatever reason, I was spared from some of that, or at least the worst of it. Not to say that I don't still embody misogyny in a lot of significant ways. I definitely do. I have noticed the ways other people have noticed that I show up as a man—as a Black man in particular, as a straight Black man especially.

There is something I know I've learned from my family about what masculinity looks like. What being present in relationships—whether platonic or romantic—with women looks like. I feel like I've learned something that a lot of Black men have missed out on for whatever reason, and I know that has to do with the way that I was raised and my interactions with my sisters.

I don't know exactly what happened or how it happened, but I think I've had a much better head start in terms of unlearning misogyny, specifically misogynoir, than most other Black men. I've never sat down and tried to figure out or articulate what those factors were or what the defining moments for me were. But yeah, there is something there. There's something there.

On Authority

Gosh, I used to know of the existence of Divine by way of authority, but now that's not really a thing anymore. I don't know how much I know by way of authority anymore. I don't trust a lot of authority outside of, I guess, people in the academy. I don't really trust lawmakers. When I was younger, parents were definitely a big thing. I really can't think of what I still know as a result of what I learned from the authority figures in my life, whether they be teachers or parents.

I don't think authority is a great teacher. I don't know that I really know anything because of authority like that anymore, at least, not viscerally. Most of what I know because of authority is stuff that I can't necessarily verify myself outside of it. Like the people that are actually on the ground in Palestine—people that are living the mess, having to do it.

Most of what I know by authority isn't stuff that I really know, but just stuff that I have to trust in because I do not have the expertise that they have. It is stuff like the earth being round or the earth not being the center of the universe. I don't totally understand how astronomy works. I didn't invent the telescope. I am not Galileo.

One of the big reasons that I know that the earth is not flat, or the earth is not the center of the universe, is because of scientists. That is stuff I know because of authority, and even still, I think that knowledge is suspect because I do not necessarily have the capacity myself without learning the math to figure that stuff out. If there's anything I know by authority, it's usually truths like that—the earth not being the center of the universe and the earth being round.

On Reason

One of those things [I know through reason] is probably—if there is a God—that God is not omnipotent or omniscient, necessarily. I reason that if God is loving, then God's lack of intervention in the evils of the world is not because God *will not* so much as God *cannot*. I reason, for example, that God is not omnipotent because a God that chooses to intervene constructively in some instances and not in others is a partial God. That's not quite the God that we're supposed to worship in Christianity.

Also, the scriptures don't actually make that claim that God is omnipotent. There's also that whole thing going on. If I've got to use both experience and what I observe in the sacred text to say what I know about God, it's that I know that God is not omnipotent based on both my experience, and what I observed in the text, and what I'm able to reason out myself.

God doesn't work like that. God is not all powerful. God cannot intervene in everything because that is just not how God operates. That is more of a reasoning thing. I feel like I know that through experience, as well, but it's mostly a reasoning thing.

We already talked about racism. I know that through lived experience, but I also know that rationally as well. I can readily observe the data that exists and conclude that racism exists because of how the data shows up. This is, I guess, still mostly observable, but this is me analyzing data and reasoning that racism is, in fact, a reality. It's one that I could observe even without having experienced it. I can look at what the data says and reason that something like racism exists.

This is a harder one, too, because I feel like what I know by way of reason isn't necessarily things that I know viscerally or deep within my body. These tend to be more shallow truths, for lack of a better phrase. Things that can be mathematically or logically deduced, things that I can know by way of "premise, conclusion," that kind of thing.

Arguments—not to say that they aren't truths that matter, but they are ones that do not exist on such a foundational or core level that I deem them important to my existence. [They are] more important to how I show up or exist in the world, to some extent. [Reason] helps me interact with other people. It helps me operate in my different jobs, but it doesn't give me the will to live, for lack of a better word.

I don't think I needed to do all that stuff that Descartes did in order to find meaning in life. I don't think I needed to logically deduce that I exist simply because I think using all the stuff that he did. That doesn't really matter to me.

I mean, it's important discourse. Don't get me wrong; I think that what Descartes did was important. But at the same time, I'm just like, "I never would've done all that." I also would not have had time to do all that—him and that nigga Kant. Those are the two most ready examples I got right now, because those are two things I think about all the time — God and racism.

On Experience

What do I know empirically? I feel like there's a lot of things, but nothing horribly important comes to mind that I haven't already named. These are things that tend to be more personal or more viscerally known.

The things that I know empirically might be the things that I know the strongest. Even still, that can be challenged a little bit because not everybody can know the things that I know empirically. For example, my knowledge of the existence of the Divine. That is not something you can empirically know in the same way that I empirically know it. I know that I've had experiences, and I know that I have observed things, but these are not things that are observable in the same way to other people.

I know that religious pluralism is a thing that we have to seriously entertain. I don't know that the same way that other people would come to know it. I feel like I know that empirically, but other people know it rationally.

Of course, you have to make room for religious pluralism! If you just look at the different religions' or faith practices' capacity for saint-making, you have to make room for pluralism. Nobody's making more saints than anybody else. I can see your Gandhi with my Mother Teresa. I can see your Whatever Villain with my Hitler. I can rationally talk about that, but I guess I can empirically know that too. Or at least argue for it.

I empirically know it simply because I've observed sainthood. I've observed things. I've observed love or capacity for well-doing in saint-making and places and faiths outside of my own. I've seen people lean better into the precepts of Christianity who were not Christian at all than people in my own faith.

I think Gandhi may have been one of the greatest Christians to ever live, and he's not even a real Christian. That's one of the ways in which I'm able to rationalize my knowledge of religious pluralism rather than one that's more exclusive or partially inclusive. I guess that's more of an empirical thing because that is ultimately something that I could observe, but I can rationalize that too.

On Intuition

I guess this is where empiricism and intuition differ, because the implication of empiricism is that anybody would be able to observe what I'm able to observe through the senses. I don't necessarily know of God through the senses. I intuit God, I intuit the Divine. I intuit primarily the Divine. I think if there's anything that I know, mostly by intuition, it's the Divine.

I can also intuit other things. I feel like I can intuit [which] people are worth pouring into. I know where my energy is best spent in terms of how I love others, [which] people are worth pouring into in terms of my love or in terms of my time. I can intuit when somebody does not love me or when somebody does not think I'm worth the time. I feel like I know through intuition when someone needs help of some kind.

These are not things that I know from observation alone. I feel like I know them primarily through intuition. Or maybe I am observing things, but I don't really have ways to articulate, "Oh, somebody's tone changed," or "Somebody's eyes looked different," or "The light is not on in somebody's eyes." How do you articulate that observation? I don't feel like that is necessarily something that I'm empirically observing so much as I'm intuiting based on maybe what I observed. I don't totally know.

If there's anything that I'm intuiting more than observing, it is the existence of the Divine. Also, the feelings that somebody has for me in terms of how they value me and how I need to show up for them, or when they have needs that I can speak to. I feel like I know when people have a need that I can fill. That's the kind of thing I am able to know by intuition.

I can intuit when a situation or any kind of relationship is unhealthy. That is the kind of thing I can know. I feel I can also intuit when I need to move, if that makes any sense. When I need to make certain moves in life. When I'm being lured to a certain action or outcome, I feel like I can understand when I am being beckoned to move.

What I know through intuition is when it is time to move on to a different activity, to a different person, into a certain course of action. I mean, coming to divinity school was one of those things. Deciding not to get a PhD was one of those things. I guess—to put a bow on it—is of the Divine, how to move in relationship with other people and how to make moves through life with regards to relationships or activities.

On Social Cognition

[I know] that everybody's needs are valid. I think one of the most important truths I know through social cognition. This may help me make sense of my own religious beliefs or whatever, but I feel like one of the biggest things that I know through social cognition is other people's needs are holy.

In a weird way, I feel like that is the most fundamental Christian ethic—to treat other people's needs as holy. I think the primary thing I know through social cognition is that just because I don't understand other people's needs doesn't mean they're not valid or even sacred. I would say that's the primary thing I know through social cognition. What people need is sacred, is holy.

On Balancing Ways of Knowing

I'd love to say that I operate more on experience than anything—or reason—but I don't know how true that is. They definitely play a role, but, ultimately, I feel like I pay a lot of attention to my intuition. If there's any way in which I move, I feel like I pay attention most to my intuition.

I think I give voice or give most control to my experience. Intuition can tell me things that I just will not listen to because I don't want to. Because of my experience, I know that I have a lot of abandonment issues, and I'll move accordingly. I've noticed how that has shown up in the way that I attach myself to other people. I revert to a lot of people pleasing behaviors if I even feel like I'm about to get abandoned, and that's not an intuition thing. That's more of an experience thing.

Experience has taught me that if I act in a certain way or if I move in a certain way, people will abandon me. I know that my default behavior to please other people is a result of my experience, not so much as my intuition. I can know that a situation is not good for me or reason that a situation is not good for me, but I still act according to my experience because of that. I would probably have to say that I default most to experience.

On Passing Things on to Family

I don't feel like I've tried to pass anything on because—as the self-proclaimed dumbest sibling in the family—I don't feel like there's anything worth passing on, so much as absorbing. I don't feel like I've needed to pass on anything that my sisters don't already know or haven't already figured out for themselves. There's no work to be done among my siblings. Maybe to Mom and Dad, which I guess plays a part in why I'm seeing both of them this holiday season and not everybody else in Utah or wherever else they go.

I also don't really have a strong desire to have kids, so there's not really any desire to pass on anything there. If I was having kids, I would really want to instill a knowledge of self-worth. Not just self-worth, but knowing that you are enough. These are things that I know to be true, but I don't live into the way that I ought to. I will be battling a feeling of being enough until I die.

If there's anything that I would want to pass on or anything I would want to make sure that I instilled in my family, it's a sense of self-worth. That you are worthy of every single need that you have, and even ones that you deserve, not just to survive, but to flourish. Also, that to be an individual is not to be an isolation. To be an individual is a communal existence. To be human is to find the best ways to live in community. I think that is the most important piece of information that I would want to pass on to my family.

On Flow

It's the closest thing to ultra instinct I'll ever experience. It takes me a little while to get to that state. I don't know how long it takes people—maybe like 20 minutes, half an hour, I don't know. But it takes me a minute to get there.

In the flow state, I am not capable of being distracted. I am capable of thinking continuously, if that makes sense. I don't experience blocks of any kind. I can just continue working. I can continue focusing in my flow states. The way I experience them is an ability to maintain and also want to maintain focus. It's not difficult for me. I don't have to fight to do it, and I'm also not thinking about my capabilities or abilities; I just do.

There are certain thoughts that are non-existent anymore, certain insecurities that are not present anymore. It is just a state where I'm just able to do and just able to exist and able to focus. It's hard to describe, I guess. When I experience flow, those are the primary things that I take note of, simply because they are not my default. They're not things that I feel come naturally to me, an ability to keep continuous focus, to keep continuous thought processes going, to keep continuous work going, and to not be self-conscious about my abilities. That is probably the most notable thing about flow state for me.

Being alone is a big one for sure [to create flow]. Being in a space where I'm comfortable. Being in my apartment is a big part of it. I mean, if my apartment's just clean, or if I'm just post-cleaning in my apartment, that's when I notice I'm most likely to enter the flow state. Because I'm already on a string of productive things, and I can keep it going with my work. Or—weird enough—also just after I have recovered by either watching a TV show or playing a video game when my mind is refreshed or rested, but also still stimulated. I can enter the flow state that way, and I can enter it quicker.

Those are not things that I consciously do. These are just things that are like, "Okay, I need to not think so hard for a while. Let me engage in some light mentally stimulating activity or watching a TV show or playing 2K, and then let me get back to my work." Then I'll be able to enter the flow state faster because the desire to work is higher, and also the ability to go harder.

There's not a lot of conscious things I do other than just make sure my work area is clean. Most of the stuff that I do to get there is unconscious. I started taking Adderall recently, too, so that's one of the conscious things I do—taking my drugs and cleaning my room.

Jette with her husband Jake and daughter Nora

Jette Jones Laughlin is a licensed clinical social worker in Texas. She works in a hospital system and also sees clients in her private practice. She and her family (including their dog, Louie) enjoy going on walks and visiting with friends and family.

18

JETTE

This chapter includes excerpts from my interview with my sister, Jette Jones Laughlin.

~

On What She Knows

I guess when you know something, you feel it. It's something that your brain has held onto and decided is right, and that's what you base your decisions off of. I think love always finds a way into your life one way or another. Everybody is deserving of some form of love, whether or not they want it. I think it's wrong to intentionally hurt people. We should always be trying to give dignity to others, if we have any control over it. I do think there's a God out there, something that's over all this chaos. I don't know where He is, but He's out there somewhere. Or She.

I think people who end up hurting other people are, I guess you could say, failing in life. I think there's a hole in their heart somewhere. I'm not saying that we're all responsible for filling that, but I think the only way to really over-come those holes is to fill them with good.

I think it should be part of everybody's mission to try and do good and uplift others. Or at least not harm them, because life will do that. We don't have to try to hurt other people. Ultimately, we'll end up playing ourselves and getting hurt.

I think I've seen in my own experience when I have taken the extra energy to try to be ugly to somebody, some-where it comes back down the line. I guess it's karma or whatever you want to call it. And I'm like, "Man, maybe I should have not done that." But when I'm nice, even when somebody has been ugly to me, I feel like it comes back around to them naturally. I mean, they're going to have something that's going to bite them in the butt, eventually. Whether or not I'm there to see it, I just know it's going to happen.

I just figure, "Well, I may as well just be nice because that'll help me. It'll be beneficial to me. Ultimately, the other person's going to get what they end up putting out." That's been my experience, so I really do think that's true.

On Family Influence

Growing up in a fairly large family, I'd always had some-body who I assumed—and I think knew—also cared about me. I had 4 siblings and then 2 parents. There was always somebody—even if I didn't feel like I got along well with somebody else—there was always someone there who was kind to me and would lift me up. From that, I learned that there is always love in our lives, whether or not we're looking for it intentionally. On the love part, that influenced that, I suppose.

Of course, we grew up in a Christian household, so that influenced my beliefs on whether or not God is there. That definitely that influenced it, and I'm glad for that. I'm glad I grew up in a house that was Christian. Whether or not we were following that super well all the time, having that good foundation of principles to base my life on was good for me. Having the adults at church who were caring and kind, I think that was very impactful for me, in addition to having parents who were involved. All those positive influences from adults at church and what have you, I think that was impactful.

I think I needed to be able to get out on my own to really be able to flourish and grow. I don't think I could have if I were close to home because I had to differentiate between what others were telling me I should be and what I felt I needed to do. I had to be in a place where nobody knew me or knew much about me so I could prove to myself what I wanted to be and felt I needed to be was true and was possible.

On Authority

LaShawn definitely gave me a big Black history lesson that I did not ever get when I was in 7th grade. I never will forget that because when I taught that to my class, even my teacher was just like, "I want you to teach this to the next class." And then I did. I wouldn't have known if nobody had told me.

She taught me that slaves were brought over from Africa, and they were brought to three different continents, actually—Europe, South America, and [North] America. I learned African roots were very strong in South America because they had the fresher crops of slaves. They kept killing them, which is really brutal.

Particularly, what stuck with me was how when we came to [North] America, it was not that we were necessarily treated better, but the way that they divided up slaves made it harder for us to keep our heritage. Because they separated us by families. They separated families, and there was no real connection to the African culture because there was an intentional effort to destroy the connections to any heritage we had, really.

We're called African Americans because nobody really knows where we're from except for Africa. There's no real connection to our tribes and what have you, and it's hard to trace any of our lineage back. Yeah, I learned that. Nobody explained that to me.

On Reason

I guess I knew I was supposed to marry Jake by way of reason and logic. Because in addition to feeling good about it, of course, I wouldn't have [married him] if I had just done what somebody told me. Which is to marry somebody in the [LDS] temple and what have you. I wouldn't have married him, but I did anyways because, logically, it was just like, "Well, if it's not him, then who?" I went ahead and got married to him, regardless of what the authorities said.

On Experience

Through experience, I think ultimately I am responsible for myself. Particularly post high school, as a technical adult. I had to be responsible for my bills, paying rent. Once I had to have more financial responsibility, I understood what the value of a dollar was, and how far it really goes, and how quickly it goes.

I learned when it comes to being responsible for my body, what that really looks like. When it comes to exercising and eating, not eating a piece of cake in the middle of the day at noon so that I can have enough energy to stay awake. Those kinds of things—like being responsible—I had to learn that through experience because I did it the wrong way, I guess is what I'm saying.

I had to go into debt on spending money on silly things when I was in undergrad[uate] school to realize I don't have to spend money and go into debt or use my credit card really at all. If I don't have the money to buy something, I could just wait and do it later when I have enough money. Or I can wait to eat the piece of cake that I want after I've been productive in the day, and then I can treat myself with it later so that I'm not tired when I need to do something important because I have a sugar hangover.

Also, of course, starting early on homework assignments. Realizing if it's complicated, and I can't get it after a couple days of thinking and ruminating on it, I need to ask for help. These are things I learned through experience, because I didn't always do those things the right way.

On Intuition

I've always known I was supposed to have kids. I like being a mom. I just always have felt that I was supposed to do that at some point.

It's annoying to admit this. Growing up as a little Black girl or young Black woman, people always tell you that you're going to be independent and are going to be able to be strong and take care of everything. I also had the thought that I was just going to be a submissive housewife. I also kind of knew that was never going to be my role. I guess I've always just kind of known I could end up in the situation I'm in now, which is, I'm a breadwinner.

I always knew I needed to go to school, even though I didn't enjoy school very much. I always knew I was going to have to go and make sure I had my credentials or whatever so that I could take care of not just myself, but my whole family. I always knew that I was going to have to do it, so I just went ahead and did it, even though I didn't want to.

On Social Cognition

I think people will tell you what they think you want to hear. When it comes to doing surveys and stuff like that, I don't think those are 100% reliable because I think people hide their true feelings. I think a big part of interacting with people is getting to really know them as a person.

They'll tell you, for example, that they missed your party because they had something come up or because they had to go take the kids to school or something. But they really, maybe, just didn't want to go, and they're just not telling you that. I think people will tell you what they think you want to hear if they don't really trust you and feel safe with you as a person. In that case, maybe they'll tell you the truth.

When it comes to being female, I know at this point I am not seen as equal to a male. I just kind of accepted that. It sucks, but I know because the people I interact with—they're often trying to validate something I said by talking to somebody else who's either male or white. I'm just like, "Well, okay then, as long as I'm getting my money, I guess I'll accept this treatment." I know that because of my interactions with others. That's how people see me. It's not how I see myself, to be clear.

Sometimes, if I need something, I have to tell somebody

that I need it instead of asking for it. There's a way to ask for something and make sure that you get it. For example, I requested Christmas off and didn't get it. I requested it off twice, and I was being nice and trying not to be too assertive. Then I told them that I needed the week after Christmas off and they gave it to me. You got to tell people what you need, and then they'll give it to you or they won't. If they don't, you go somewhere else for it.

On Balancing Ways of Knowing

I mean, I definitely think experience [is what I lean on most]. If something has gone well for me, then I keep doing that thing. I think experience more so than authority. We grew up with lots of authority figures in our life. I mean, we were in a military family, and then we also had the church. Experience, logic, reason, and social cognition. There we go.

On Passing Things on to Family

It seemed to really hurt Morgan that Dad wouldn't come to her wedding or what have you, and I was kind of like, "You're an adult now. You've got to make these decisions and just go with them. You can't really make everybody happy." Sometimes you just got to go ahead and do what's right for you, regardless of what other people say, even if it's your own family.

On Flow

Gosh, it's hard with phones and everything, how to sift that out. I feel like when I'm planning something, I'm usually using my phone. That's kind of trippy to think about. Like, is my phone putting me in a flow state, or am I putting me in a flow state?

I get quiet. I notice I have to think about things a lot. I can be sitting on the couch, and Jake will be like, "Are you okay?" And I'm like, "Yeah, I'm fine." But I really just am thinking. I consider that part of my flow too, because I have to think about things, and they have to make sense in my head. I have to play out different scenarios before I can take my action. I don't have to have another person do that. I can just do that by myself. If I'm just sitting on the couch and quiet and just zoning out, I would consider that my flow state.

Being outside, being able to walk around, that helps. Just not having anywhere in particular to go. Just being able to be like, "Okay, I'm going to walk, and I'm going to walk as long as I want." That's helpful.

I think cooking a meal or something that helps me to be just in a flow state, I suppose. Because I'm focusing on something and saying I'm completing it from beginning to end. I think having good sleep also helps. Being able to go to bed, think about things, sleep, then wake up in the morning. That's a good way to get me ready to be in a flow state. And also planning lists out, putting things to do on my lists. I like doing that.

Morgan (left) and her spouse, Taylor

Morgan Jones Yarbrough recently received a master's degree in learning experience design and educational technology. She has several years' experience in customer service and administrative support. She and her spouse Taylor are the proud dog parents of Mellie and Sage.

19

MORGAN

This chapter includes excerpts from my interview with my sister,
Morgan Jones Yarbrough.

❦

On What She Knows for Sure

For my core beliefs, I feel like love is love. I feel like you are allowed to love whomever you want, whoever you love. There's not a moral issue with that. Of course, if minors, non-consent, abhorrent and illegal things like that are the topic, then I'm like, "No, absolutely not. We're not doing that." There's that.

I want to say I was definitely a single digit age [when I knew love is love]. I was pretty young, and Mom and Dad were having an argument about women being on the front lines of war. It was a very random situation, and there was something going on in the news about women in the military, then, the next topic after that was gay men and gay women in the military. Mom just said things that made me feel very uncomfortable, and Dad was just, like, "Well, if they want to serve the country, I don't see what's wrong with that." I was just thinking about that as a whole—what does somebody's sexual orientation have to do with their ability to serve the country?

Outside of that, I felt uncomfortable with people being gay/queer/not straight being seen as a negative thing. There are people who exist who love who they love and are seen as weak because of that? It's really dehumanizing.

I was more intrigued by it, and looking back at those times I feel even more that I was comfortable with and curious about same sex attraction because I fell into those categories. In those moments, I was like, "Oh yeah, we love gays. This is great. This seems normal and good, and I would love to see more of it." I've just kind of felt that way ever since I can remember. I feel like it's a mixture of me feeling uncomfortable with people expressing negative opinions about same-sex attracted people. They are people, too, and there's not anything wrong there. I felt very affirmed seeing same-sex couples, reading about them, and experiencing them in person, even though I didn't understand my sexuality really at the time.

I also believe that we should be able to make decisions about our own bodies, and that's not something that somebody else gets to do for us. Of course, there are some situations where if we can't take care of ourselves, and we appoint somebody to make decisions for us legally—but outside of that, no thank you.

I believe that there are people who need financial support outside of us and that we should be able to have some kind of system set up to help people. I guess taxes go toward some of those needs at this time. So, I think that's okay. I don't think that needs to not be a thing. Very glad fundraising is a virtual platform as well because there are so many people willing to help others financially in times of need, and to support passion projects like a business, or non-profit organization, etc.

On Family Influence

Growing up, I was very interested in what adults were doing because I was around adults a lot. For the most part, I would do anything to be around Mom or Dad or anybody who would rear me, mostly. I listened to a lot of the things that they said. I had a very deep interest in knowing what they thought and what kinds of things seemed important to them to expect from us as children.

I think that they definitely were a really prominent base in how they influenced me because, naturally, I was stuck to somebody, whether I was with Mom or Dad or LaShawn or maybe a friend's parents or something like that. I am the youngest of 5, so I would just be around people older than me all the time. They'd have phone conversations that I would hear. They'd be with their spouses or other adults talking, and I would just hear the types of things that they would think, and with context clues, I could have an idea, from a child's perspective, of what is important to people who are important to me, and I would incorporate those things into my daily thoughts and actions.

One thing that I forgot about was religion, too. It was something that was always around. It's something that's regularly within the household in my daily life, so I just experienced religion-based behaviors, teachings, and principles repeatedly. There really wasn't any escaping it, and in a lot of ways now it do be feeling inescapable. Church and state are....not separated. We (me [giggle]) are deconstructing from a repressive religious upbringing currently, so we are v[ery] tender about a lot of this stuff still. So much good, but so much more harm, I'm afraid.

I would say they didn't use these words, but they would instill race as a social construct in me regularly, especially as I began to ask questions about race. I think about that every day and find that to be very true. A lot of things that have to do with being a little Black girl, just having to try twice as hard anyway because I'm black. But then, because I'm a woman, it's three times as hard, and then coming out as queer, it's four times as hard. And then, in an interracial relationship, five times as hard. In the South, a very conservative place, six times as hard. Those types of things. I believe these things and think about them regularly, and most days, it's less bleak to navigate, and other days, it gets pretty depressing.

With education—which is also something that is a core value I did not bring up earlier—they've taught me that having education is very important because of the previous things that I mentioned being against me in social, political, financial constructs. Having an education would put me in a different zone of opportunity, if that's a good way to describe that opportunity for comfort above survival.

They've taught me that I'm a good person, also in my core beliefs. I think I have a lot of shame, unfortunately, because of other core things that were brought into my life that have hurt me over time. They've always told me that I'm a good person, that I'm lovable, that I have very desirable attributes, things like that. That's helped me feel good or maybe helped me come back to the center when I'm feeling very shameful and ugly inside, which is impactful. I would probably say something else they've taught me that I believe to be true is that when somebody shows you who they are, you need to believe them. I mean, there have been too many situations where that's been true with myself, personally—me [with] me and me with other people.

On Authority

Well, something that's very fresh in my brain because I'm always looking into this and reading up on it has to do with nails, LOL. There are a lot of professionals that I've followed for years. I know things based on different classes and videos that I've taken and watched that they've provided, which I've then applied to my own practices when doing nails.

I have an undergraduate degree in sociology, so I've learned a lot of contemporary and classical theorists' interesting pearls of wisdom that they've imparted via theory and concepts that they've shared. Switching gears a bit, I have two dogs, so I look up behavioral information from training authorities on how to work with dogs, train, and understand them. There are things that I know by way of authority from those experts, I suppose you could say.

I tend to be a very trusting person, and authority has been tricky in many ways for me throughout my life. I think authority has positives and negatives, and even in situations where you feel like you can trust an authority, it is important to ensure you have done ample research and feel confident in placing your trust in someone/something as an authority. Also, do your best to feel confident to advocate for yourself and ask questions or do things that allow you to get what you need and, hopefully, what you want.

On Reason

There are a lot of things that don't be making sense to me. Right now, with Palestine and Israel, I'm like, "Why are we funding the complete depletion of and hurting and depriving basic human life from Palestinian people? Why are we hurting people who did not ask for or want any of this? They have nothing to do with the actual terrorism that is going on, and we just need not be doing all this. Ceasefire permanently. NOW. Thank you so much." I have been so sick over this and could go on a tirade, but I want to end by saying that what is being done to Palestine and Gaza is not okay.

Also, because I live in the South and have two Southern parents, other things that I feel like I know by way of reason is that it really, honestly, truly, authentically, and allegedly should not make a difference what somebody looks like in any situation at all, ever. For some reason, it does. Well, I mean, for multiple reasons, it does. I just feel like it's very o out of 10. We have to do better as a whole regarding addressing our biases and prejudices. A discussion for another day, perhaps!

It just isn't reasonable that people are judged and discriminated by the whole because of their skin color, based on their sexual orientation, who they're with. They're judged on if they have any level of education. Just judgments that have to do with perceived successes and accolades. [That doesn't] make sense to me because people are wildcards and just because they have an education does not mean that they will not run your business into the ground.

By way of reason and experience, honestly, one good thing that I can think of, too, is that just because somebody did something that you are doing and they found it to be easy does not mean that it is, in fact, going to be easy for you to do. Or that it's attainable. That's applicable in so many areas of life.

I think I'd like to add that it's reasonable to expect people to have changed, and also reasonable to expect them to have not changed at the same time. We are not exclusively just one or the other, we can be both, and. Allowing others that flexibility of growth and change with their journeys, and allowing that for ourselves too is important, v[ery] reasonable, even!

On Experience

You just don't always know how you're going to feel about something [new] until you're experiencing [it]. There is a general sense that I can tell I am probably going to feel some kind of way about something, but I really won't know until I'm actually doing that something. That's important.

I know how each day will be because my schedule is mostly the same every day, unless I have something planned that I know is going to be a little bit different. I can plan differently by experience. I can essentially plan for new things in my schedule, and it's not going to throw me off because I know what my every day is. Adding something in that's new, I can plan for that and manage my time appropriately based on changes. I will let you know once I've mastered that though [because] executive function is a struggle for me.

One thing I'm learning to do is time management with the different nail services that I'm offering. I guess that's a new thing, too, with experience. I know how long it takes me to do certain things, whether it's a gel application or structured gel manicure, or cuticle work or nail art, stuff like that. I can give a very accurate time on how long I take to do things based on how long it's taken me to do them over and over.

I think you can get a lot further with actively listening to somebody when they're talking with you versus analyzing everything that they're saying immediately and holding on to different ways that you would respond to them. That's something that's useful in a lot of different situations. I find that through experience; I've definitely gotten a lot further actively listening instead of just interrupting and spouting out different things that I'm thinking of as they're talking. It do be hard to not spout out though because [of] ADHD, but that's another story!

I know by way of experience that people are judgmental regarding what religion you are, what race you are, what level of education you have, what job you have, how much money you make. Yeah, unfortunately, those types of judgments are definitely everywhere all the time. At least, they are here.

Another thing that I know by way of experience is that I'm capable of doing things that make people feel happy but also that make people feel sad or supported, unsupported or worried or insecure, etc. It's a lot of power, so I do my best to be responsible with what I do and say.

On Intuition

While I think logically and tend to intellectualize my feelings, you can also find me like, "The vibes are not immaculate. The vibes are off." I would say, by way of intuition, I know that there are ways to infer a lot about somebody without necessarily having a lot of time spent with them. I've been able to infer a lot about people within minutes of meeting them, and it's not necessarily because they told me their life story--though sometimes they do tell me their life stories, bless it. They could appear tense, anxious, or generally at ease, or something like that.

Those same intuitive traits help me discern when to engage and when to not engage with certain topics. Sometimes, people just want to be heard and talk with no real discussion. It could be best to listen and affirm when safety is a concern. There have been a lot of times when white people I know and white people I don't know have approached me and asked me questions about Black children they've adopted or about perceptions of Black peoples' experiences, just to tell me what they think and talk over me. It's weird, but sometimes I would rather let them talk than answer them when they don't really want to discuss and understand my perspective—even though they asked me for my perspective. Chileee, [I don't know]. They feel they've got it, and that's their prerogative, I guess.

There are feelings that I feel if I enter an area or space that's just not for me. There's just a heaviness that I can feel physiologically when in spaces that can kind of allow me to decide, "Do I need to stay here and be to myself, or do I need to stay here and change something about this air, or do I need to leave?" I also feel when people are not in the best moods. I feel the same kind of heaviness in my chest, shoulders, and neck, even if they're not saying anything negative. The ways that they interact with things and people around them can be indicative of their moods.

Even in the moment, if it's the first time I've ever experienced something, I can just tell how somebody's feeling and make decisions on whether or not this is something I need to involve myself in to assist and help them figure out what's going on, or if I need to leave, which is very confusing as a child. I say 'as a child' because my childhood is when I began noticing those feelings from others. Very off-putting as a child to notice adults having dysregulated emotions and basically expect me to do something about their feelings or fix the situation or whatever. As an adult, it's confusing, too, honestly. The way my body and emotional self have held onto those feelings is something else. It's probably trauma— let's be so for real. [chuckle]

On Social Cognition

By way of social cognition, I can know where I stand or where I fit in a social situation. If I am walking into, let's say, somebody's birthday, and it's somebody that I know enough about. They're a coworker. Maybe I know that they're conservative, so I might assume more conservative people will be at this event. I may feel a bit awkward going into the party because I'm unsure if I'll have similar views as guests to where we can get along, but I know that once I'm actually there, I can continually check in with myself as I'm among guests, and I'll enjoy the cake and company. I can get by in a lot of situations like this; I can notice general behavior— who sits where, how loud or quiet is it, has anyone started eating yet, are children here, the list goes on—dress, talking points, social mores we abide by and decide how I can present where I am.

There are a lot of things I think I've understood by way of social cognition in terms of safety for me or other people. Just being [truly] accepted somewhere. I think on a shallow level, maybe I can feel accepted and find some places. As a whole, if I were to look into it a little more, I could under-stand, yeah, it'd be fine for me to be in this conservative space probably. But I'm not sure how I could be perceived and treated because of my race, sexuality and gender if I am by myself. That's probably something that I think about a lot, honestly; what do I represent in this space that I'm in to the people that I'm around? What does that mean for me in terms of safety and value probably would be something that's very relevant every day in those social situations.

On Balancing Ways of Knowing, Leaning on Certain Ways of Knowing

I feel like I mostly work with a mixture of all of the ways of knowing continuously, maybe seamlessly moving between them, and using them concurrently, especially leaning on some more than others depending on how I'm feeling. Maybe I lead more with experience and intuition and reason more when dealing with new situations or meeting new people, but the more I think about it, I, maybe, use authority less because I don't know a lot of stuff and feel uncomfortable claiming authority within a space because of that. I'm working on that, haha. Authority doesn't mean you know everything, but you know enough to feel confident in how you contribute. That can be a very useful and important flex and credential in the right spaces and situations, ya know?

Much like life, it goes on. You learn new things about things you already thought you learned and knew about. And the same goes for ways of knowing. Everything is connected, just like we're all connected on this wave. We're weaving all of these ways of knowing into the fabric—into the filter, as it were—and we love to see it.

On Passing Things on to Family

I feel like I'm an absolute clown with my family. As far as passing knowledge, I just don't know that I really pass knowledge to them, to be honest. I love teaching and talking about and discussing all the things with you and Mom and LaShawn, family, friends, anyone who wants to listen, really.

I think with nail artistry things, I definitely am very 12 out of 10 with imparting my feels to the family about that. With crystals and things like that, I've always really liked that kind of stuff. With spiritual properties, and then with Tarot and stuff — when I lived with LaShawn, I would do readings on myself, and I would do readings for Jordan, one of my besties. I would have my crystals and just have them set up different places, and LaShawn would have a lot of questions about that. We hadn't really gotten into it with her past with it or anything like that, but I'm thinking about it now and I'm just grateful that she was more curious about it instead of, "It's literally brujeria." I love that.

I don't know if that's family as a whole, but LaShawn is family, so I think that can count as family as a whole. Not sure if that made her feel any specific type of way about it now, but I at least know she's not negative about it. She seems to be very welcoming of it, and that's nice. I can't say if that's because of me, but I would hope that I helped spark something for her to continue to be okay with it.

Also, maybe experience with me being not straight, with being queer. If anybody ever has questions, or if I'm sharing different things about my experiences being in a queer relationship or trying to make connections with people as somebody who's queer in more conservative spaces, just my lived experience. A knowledge of that can be indirectly shared. I don't know that it's stuff that I've tried to pass on to

anybody. Not that I avoid doing that, but I don't intentionally try to do that.

Maybe I can pass on my experiences. I can pass on life
moments that were meaningful to me, that they may be able
to relate to at some point, or many points. I think a lot of the
questions you've asked can be connected with each other,
which I'm just now noticing! That's cool!

On Flow

I don't know if me being fixated on something and getting
into it is the same thing or not. The closest thing that I can
think of to a flow state is being fixated or hyper fixated on
something and having no concept of time, which really is
not practical at times.

I guess I just really experience it by finding the end of a
string, so to speak, and starting to pull it. When I've pulled
the end of the string and it's unraveling whatever I'm doing
or thinking to where I'm like, "Oh, yeah, yeah, yeah, that's
it," I just keep pulling. The continued pulling is me making
progress through the flow state, where I'm able to capture
what is getting me to the point and full understanding, step-
by-step, of what I'm doing, so I can work through it until I'm
at the end, and the task is complete.

When I'm mentally prepared to get into what I'm
working on, I've removed the unnecessary things that are
preventing me from actually getting into what I'm doing. My
mind can have a lot going on, especially when it comes to It
can be taking me hours sometimes to just get into a focused,
"getting things done" state of mind, which is unfortunate.

Because my brain thinks several miles an hour, I really
have to get all of my wiggles out of my body. Let's say I'm
sitting down, and I'm doing this assignment, but dishes need

to be done and that is occupying my mind. I'll just go and do the dishes, and then I'll be like, "Okay, yeah, actually that was very helpful." I'm not thinking about that anymore. I can actually have some bandwidth and brain space to give to what's important for me to get done right now with less distraction.

Sometimes, it's me physically doing something, and then other times, maybe I just have a lot on my brain. I mean, doing dishes isn't super important. Sometimes, I'm just like, "Yes, I do need to do dishes, but I don't need to do them right now," so I will have to take some time and meditate or just breathe. Focusing on my breathing and just allowing myself to actually breathe, instead of being so tensed with all these things that I think I should be doing. That helps a lot. I just feel so much more relaxed when I can do that. Some kind of breathing meditation can be helpful.

Dishes are surface level, though they can feel overwhelming when I have other things that are deeper and feel big sometimes: How are my relationships? How's my marriage?" Am I feeling like I've been a good partner lately, or friend, or sibling, daughter, etc.? Do I feel like I am a good person, or like I'm safe in my body and soul? Have I offended or hurt someone and are they struggling because of this?" These kinds of things can creep up on me and bury themselves into my unconscious mind and really wreak havoc when I'm having a rough day because I "haven't done the dishes" in a few days. The dishes are just the cherry on top. Look a little deeper into things that are harshing your flow! Talk with people who are willing to affirm, and validate your concerns. You are included in that! Talk with yourself, too! When you can work through some of that, your flow can be accessed with less delay, I think.

Fynn, Nalani, and Naiobi sitting in front of the Black Lit exhibit at Utah Valley University

Fynn is a high school student. He enjoys music and theatre. Fynn was recently a lead in a stage adaptation of Jane Austen's *Persuasion*.

Naiobi is attending junior high. According to her mother, she is a therapist in the making because of how she handles friend drama. She likes basketball, fashion, and my nail designs.

Nalani is in elementary school. She plays soccer and

likes watching horror movies. As you will see in her interview, she also likes unicorns.

20

FYNN, NAIOBI, AND NALANI

T his chapter includes my full group interview with
Fynn, Naiobi, and Nalani.

~

Niecie: I would like to state on the record that the last time
that I interviewed Nobi and Fynn was 10 years ago and it
was a—

Naiobi: WHAT

Niecie: Yes, I did. We were doing a [fake] news report, and
I asked you all for a comment. And what you said to me
when I asked for the comment was, "Oh, I don't know,
booty cheeks." Then you laughed, and then I told you I
would never ask you for a comment ever again.

Fynn: That sounds like us!

Niecie: So, I'm back asking [for a comment] against my better judgment. All right, so first question, what does it mean to know something?

Naiobi: It's like where you know it and—

Niecie: You can't use the word in the answer.

Naiobi: Well, to know something, it's just like, I don't know. You have to feel it, and you feel like you know it, and you feel like you're right.

Fynn: I would say to know something would probably be to make a judgment on something based on a certain experience. And to have a feeling in your heart that thing you know is right, or that judgment you make is right.

Niecie: What are some things that you feel like you know for sure?

Naiobi: I know everything, almost. I'm a really smart kid in school, so the stuff I've learned from school since I learned it.

Niecie: What do you know to be true?

Naiobi: What do I know to be true? Honestly, I don't know because everything here could be a lie, and we could be controlled by the government. You don't even know unless you are the government. Then you would know.

Nalani: I know that God is real.

Niecie: How do you know that?

Nalani: Well, I don't know it, but I have faith in it.

Fynn: I feel like I know for sure that my mom loves me and that I've got a loving family. I feel like I know this for sure because of the things that they do for me and stuff. I know for sure that I live a very privileged life compared to some other places.

Niecie: How would you say your family has influenced what you know? Anyone can answer. So, for example, when you said you know that God's real, do you feel like your family taught you that? Influenced that?

Nalani: Yes, by bringing us to church every Sunday.

Niecie: Okay. Other things? How has your family influenced what you know, Naiobi?

Naiobi: They made me go to school. That's when I learned that stuff.

Fynn: You said how has my family influenced what I know for sure? Well, what I also know for sure is how to surround myself with good people. What my family has done, especially my mom, is whenever I've come into a mishap socially, she influences what I know for sure about how people behave and what kind of people that have in my life by talking to me about these experiences that I have and how to get better kinds of people in my life.

Niecie: We're going to talk about different ways of knowing things. The first way is by authority. Someone telling you something, and you believe it's true because someone else, or a textbook, or an expert told you something.

Nalani: Church.

Fynn: What do you know from church?

Nalani: What they teach in church?

Niecie: Sure. What do you feel like you know?

Nalani: Because of church?

Niecie: Yeah.

Fynn: I'm taking a history class, an AP one especially, and I feel like a lot of things that I think I know for sure—basic events that happened during the Civil War and stuff—I feel like I only know that because I read a lot of textbooks. That, plus my teacher's words. I guess those are things that I think I know for sure, but they're only because of authorities—people who write the history books and people who are my teachers.

Niecie: Another way of knowing is by reason or logic. Do we all know what this is? Have you ever had the thought, "Well, if this thing is true, then this other thing is true?" What would be a good example? If I have a hand—and my hand has five fingers—then other people who have hands are going to have five fingers. Things like that.

Naiobi: Not always.

Niecie: That introduces a logical fallacy, which is a thing where not everyone has [five fingers], but—in general—some people will reason that.

Nalani: If I say, "If we found dinosaur fossils, then dinosaurs are real?"

Niecie: Yes! That's what reason is, that sort of thinking. Go ahead, tell me what you think   you know by reason.

Nalani: Okay, so, if we found dinosaur fossils, then that must mean dinosaurs are real.

Fynn: I mean, I mentioned earlier that I think I live a more privileged life than some. I want to use what's going on right now in Palestine, specifically. I'm like, "Okay, if these people are experiencing a lot of miserableness and war and stuff—because I know that they are; I've seen videos of it, and I'm not experiencing troubles like that—then that's how I know that I must be living a more privileged life than they are. Because I'm not experiencing stuff like that.

Niecie: Nobi, how do you approach schoolwork?

Naiobi: Basically, when I get my schoolwork, I complete it as soon as I can because I don't want to have to do it later. I get it done in school, and so I don't have to do it at my house. If I don't do it at my house, then I'll eventually do it, so then I don't forget about it and not do it.

Niecie: Do you know that because that you had to do trial and error? Do you know that because you have thought through like, "Okay, if I do it this way, that means this thing will happen and that means this thing will happen?

Naiobi: I've thought through it because I'm a busy lady, and I've seen other people that don't do their work when they first get it. The kids at my school—they won't do their work when they get it, and then they'll eventually end up not even doing it when they say they're going to do it. They get distracted, and they don't do it. Then it becomes late work. I've learned from them that I should do my work when I get it, so then I can get it done.

Niecie: It sounds like by observing or watching other people, that has informed your schoolwork process as well, which leads us into things that we know by experience or things that we know through our senses. Things that we see, that we hear, smell, taste, all those different senses. It's usually seeing or hearing. What are the things that you know through those senses? what would you say you know by experience?

Fynn: I want to use an example. Me and Nobi were at the skating rink yesterday, and we were sitting by this area that was—like, the speakers were right next to us. I noticed that my right ear was hurting really bad. I was right next to the speaker. They're really loud. I know from experience that I don't usually sit right by the speakers. I've noticed that when I sit farther away from them, the music is still pretty loud, but it's not too loud. So I know because I've gotten closer to the speakers that I don't want to be over there because I've gone through that and it wasn't fun.

Niecie: Let's talk about intuition. Do we know what that word means?

Naiobi: Your gut feeling.

Niecie: Gut feeling, yes. That is definitely a way to describe that. Intuition can also mean the things that you kind of know, but you don't directly—

Nalani: You don't have proof.

Niecie: Yes, you don't have the physical or other proof that's observable for other people to look at that and also be like, "Oh yeah, that's a thing." Do you feel like you guys have intuition? Somewhat?

Naiobi: No. Never. I don't have a gut feeling.

Niecie: Okay, Nala, did you say you didn't have it? Fynn?

Fynn: I said somewhat. What I mean by somewhat is I feel like I don't really have to face decisions where I have to use my intuition a lot. Either that or, when I do, my gut feeling doesn't really feel as strong, telling me to choose this option or choose this option. The other one is super bad. It doesn't feel as certain because I tend to overthink a lot. I'm often like, "Okay, but what about the other decision?" I don't know. I think the feeling has never been that strong. When I make decisions, my intuition has never been that concentrated, if that makes sense.

Niecie: Let's go to the last way of knowing. This one is called social cognition, and it's about your relationships with other people and how you understand other people's behavior in relationship to your own. For example, when babies are little and they're kind of reading your facial features and stuff, that's them developing their social cognition. Learning based off of how you respond, what you're thinking about them, and how they feel, how you feel about them type of thing. Does that make sense? You're probably going to notice this most with your friends and family. What are things that you've learned socially with other people based off of their behavior? Verbal and nonverbal?

Nalani: So, basically, when someone shakes their head up and down, that means yes. And if they shake their head side to side, that means no.

Niecie: Yes, yes. Any other things that you've learned through social cognition?

Naiobi: No.

Fynn: I observe a lot of body language through people sometimes when I tell them something. Or just when I'm talking to them, let's say that. Because when I'm talking to someone, I notice how I'll be engaged, and I'll be trying to give them eye contact. But if I notice that they are looking down, or if they're folding their arms, or if they're more closed in, then I notice that they might be feeling sad. I think that might be a sign whenever I see that to be like, "Okay, let me maybe stop for a second and ask, 'Hey, are you okay?'" I think that's probably something I've learned with social cognition, if that works.

Niecie: Okay, so then, here's another question. Do you feel like you pick up on social cues?

Nalani: I think I pick up on social cues pretty well.

Fynn: Reading the room is part of it.

Niecie: Yes. Reading the room, being able to understand other people's body language. Do you ever pick up on like, "Oh, I'm not getting something" or "There's something missing that I don't get," that sort of stuff?

Fynn: I think maybe a year ago, me and my mom were kind of iffy with me reading the room because sometimes I would be trying to show my mom a video on my phone and I wouldn't take a second to look and see that she was busy with something. I wasn't able to pick up on that cue that she probably wasn't open to see what I had to show her. We definitely had to talk and regroup after those moments. She was talking to me and she cares that I'm able to pick up on cues and be able to read what's going on in a room when I walk in.

Naiobi: I do because I pay attention to everything.

Niecie: Now that we remember these five [ways of knowing], which ones do you feel like you use the most in your daily life?

Naiobi: I'd say reason and social cognition.

Niecie: Why do you say that?

Naiobi: I say that because I reason about stuff every day, and I am social with everyone every day. So I have to read their social cues in order to actually interact with them because I interact with them every day.

Nalani: Yeah, I would say reasons and social cues.

Fynn: I'd say reasoning and logic, but I'd say experience, also, because I think the majority of things I know are from trial and error. Especially the more difficult things. I'll be slacking during a semester or a term, and I'll come to the test and I'll be like, "Okay, I didn't get that good of a grade on it. But I also notice that I didn't study that much. So maybe, okay, if I study next term, then I'll get a better grade on the test or if I change my habits when it comes to schoolwork." I know things based on trial and error, like experience, but I also usually reason my way through things. Even when it seems difficult, I try to think of, "Okay, what's the most logical thing that can explain why I know this is true?"

Niecie: What knowledge do you feel like you've tried to share with your family?

Naiobi: The knowledge I've tried to share with my family is time management. I tell Nala that she should do this right now because she's going to forget it later. Like, doing something now because then if you don't do it right now, then you're probably not going to get it done.

Nalani: Isn't that what ADHD is?

Niecie: What knowledge have you tried to share with your family?

Nalani: Not interrupting people and being so rude. Mostly Nobi, though.

Fynn: Something I know that I've tried to share with my family is how we sometimes wind up giving money to corporations that don't do very good things, especially when it comes to Gaza and Palestine. Even though basically say—

Naiobi: He's basically saying he wants us to starve.

Fynn: Well, this is what I mean. I'm just saying sometimes there are places that we buy from that have been known recently to give funding to genocides that go on. So I guess if that counts.

Niecie: Do you have any other things you want to share with your family?

Naiobi: I share my everyday knowledge with my family.

Niecie: Like what?

Naiobi: Everything.

Nalani: How to play Fortnite.

Naiobi: Yeah, how to play Fortnite, how to snipe someone, getting your work done on time, keeping your space clean, basic necessities and taking your own advice.

Nalani: And having manners.

Naiobi: Well, yeah, having manners.

Niecie: So, we talked about being in the flow, which means when you're very focused on something, you're not thinking about anything else, and you just feel like you're just going with it. You're in the zone; you're just doing the thing. Tell me, how do you experience that?

Naiobi: When I'm sleeping, obviously, I'm in the zone because I'm asleep. In basketball, in my games, I have to be in the zone of basketball. If I have the ball and my defender's shouting stuff in my face, I need to be in the zone, my own basketball zone—but still in the game—but zone them out. So I'm not paying attention to them, but I'm paying attention to the ball and the game.

Nalani: What was the question?

Niecie: How do you experience being in the zone and the flow?

Nalani: I've never really been in the zone.

Naiobi: You're in the zone when you're playing Roblox.

Fynn: When do you feel really concentrated?

Nalani: When I'm drawing.

Fynn: That makes sense. I've definitely felt that before when I used to draw. You're definitely kind of in your own head for a second or for a good while, actually. I have tried to get a part of a drawing really perfect, and I'm kind of like just like, "Okay, can't break focus from this. I got to go. I got to just go." And there's that. But there's also, when I'm on my phone, I seem to be kind of locked in. Social media is kind of meant to be addictive because I can just scroll forever, and I think that's what I end up doing. It's not the kind of concentration, though, where you're trying to lock in. So I think that's how I'd say I experience it in my life.

Niecie: Do you ever get in a flow with schoolwork?

Naiobi: Yeah. When I say I need to get my work done, I have to be in the zone, concentrate and focus on my schoolwork so that I can do the problem or answer the question correctly and not get distracted.

Nalani: Maybe when I'm reading books. I have to do 30 minutes of reading every day. I have this book that I really like to read. It's called Warrior Cats. I'm on the second book currently, and I usually do one chapter at a time because each chapter is really long.

Fynn: I sometimes notice that I am really focused when I'm in math, and it's one of those things where I kind of have to force myself to focus. I'll be in a lesson, and I'll be listening, and I'm like, "Okay, what he's explaining does not really make sense right now. I'm kind of lost." We'll be doing example problems or something. Once he erases this last example problem using this lesson or using this principle that I didn't pay attention to, I really got to lock in on this next problem—pay attention to what he does—

because I got to get unlost. I just got to not be confused anymore because this is going to reflect on the rest of your grades and stuff, too.

Niecie: Speaking of which, a few people in our family have talked about having ADHD. I think you talked about that, right, Nala?

Nalani: Yeah.

Niecie: Okay. So having ADHD—how does that affect your life, would you say?

Nalani: I'm not diagnosed, but my mom thinks I have ADHD. I don't know why she thinks that, but how that affects my life? Okay, so, that's a good question.

Naiobi: I know. Nala has ADHD because she can't wake up on her own. We have to actually drag her out of bed. And she can't really manage her time that well. I don't know, it's hard to explain. You just have to know. She just needs help with stuff, like cleaning her room. Becton, too, has ADHD.

Fynn: Again, I'm like Nala. I have not been diagnosed either, but I come from a very—no offense—ADHD-heavy mom. I think it reflects in my life because I'm often procrastinating, but I'm also overthinking things a lot. I think I mentioned that before. Sometimes, I struggle with completing tasks—sometimes with assignments and stuff. I think that can probably affect it. I also mentioned having to focus during school. I think I can also get distracted at times. Not really by anything in particular. That's the weird thing. You lose your train of thought kind of often. I think that can make it pretty difficult in life in a lot of ways.

Niecie: Great insight. Coming back to the flow state. Let's say you're trying to really focus on something and you need help. What are some things that help you get into that flow state—that really concentrated, focused state?

Nalani: If I'm trying to clean my room, either Mom or Nobi will come in my room and start helping me.

Fynn: When I don't know something, while I'm doing an assignment—I don't know a certain event or details about an event—I usually go to my textbook, and I try and scour for some information there. That usually gives me a little bit of a boost in what I need. Now that I have more information, then I can kind of zoom through my assignment quicker because I'm not as lost, if that makes sense. I'm not as confused because I have the context that I didn't have before.

Naiobi: I give myself motivating words by telling myself that if I can get into the zone now, then basically I get it done faster and then I won't have to do it, and then I get a victory.

Niecie: Those are all my questions. Is there anything else you feel like that's important to share at this time? Not related to booty cheeks.

Nalani: All I have to say is I like unicorns.

Niecie: Me too.

Fynn: I think this interview was very insightful, and the answers that we got from Nobi and Nala were very insightful and eye-opening as well.

Naiobi: You're welcome for my time.

21

THEMES

L istening to my family as they responded to my questions was heart-opening. I learned more about how they process things, past and present. I also saw where we have inherited many of the same social conditions and responses. I got curious about how and why we processed certain events differently, how we ended up carrying certain traumas at different levels of intensity. Whether you read all the interviews or are here for a summary, here are the themes that emerged from my family. I hope you will stay curious as you read, too.

Definition of Knowing

Several family members talked about knowing as something that feels justified based on strong belief and feeling. This makes sense, as my family tends to hold justice as a value, and feeling justified in knowledge matches up in our pursuit of balance and fairness. Feelings of certainty were also mentioned by a few people. LaShawn talked about the importance of embodying something more than just under-standing it.

What is Known and How

There were potent feelings of what is known and how those things are known. Some had to do with what is known about the self. Several family members talked about their knowledge of being loved and appreciated by self, family, and others. My mom talked specifically about her pursuit of self-care and self-love after spending most of her life caring for others. While some of this may be inherent, I also think my mom learned to adapt to others' desires for her out of survival. She lived in a time when assimilation was normal and expected of many Black people to be accepted by larger society.

Many family members talked about relational or soci-etal truths that they have learned. Much was said about the inherent worth of every person. Jette mentioned that "love always finds a way" to everyone. People talked about morals, such as the importance of treating others with kindness. I think for a lot of folks who live with identities that are outcast or not embraced, you understand the feelings that come along with it and genuinely want to spare others from feeling those in their extremities. The existence of God was mentioned several times, most notably by my dad and my youngest niece — the oldest and the youngest family members that I interviewed.

Family Influence

Socialization was the biggest way family influence was discussed. Some people talked about learning how to treat others, such as living by the "golden rule." Others talked about the understanding of race as a social construct directly and indirectly. This supports research that suggests that racial identity development begins earlier for Black people versus white people. I was probably around 7 when I was first called Black by a friend's mom. I rejected that label and instead insisted that I was "tan."

In her interview, Morgan said she came to understand that when people show you who you are, you should believe them. Along the same lines, folks talked about learning about the influence of race and racism within a family context. Additionally, knowing how to navigate bias and prejudice was influenced by family. Some people mentioned how much of this knowledge was shared indirectly versus directly, more through observation of interpersonal relationships than by other means.

Religion was also mentioned by several people. Some talked about how it was helpful to grow up in a Christian household, both for developing their understanding of the Divine and developing morals and principles for living. Jette mentioned that her religious upbringing influenced whether she believed God existed. Christianity is a strong thread that comes from both sides of my family. Both of my parents came from South Carolina and were descendants of enslaved Africans. These enslaved Africans were indoctrinated by their masters with a Christianity that preached submission but never liberation. However, the Christianity most of my family embraces now is one that focuses more on liberation, which is the case with James, who studies Black liberation theology.

Some family members mentioned ways that family created harm. Shame, anxiety, and depression were mentioned as feelings that the family environment created.

Interestingly, the experience of both being affirmed and then shamed was implied and explored in some interviews. As there was a focus on doing things as well as or better than others who might try to hold us back, this experience is understandable since there would be a focus on "punishing" behaviors seen as undesirable or bad and then "reinforcing" behaviors seen as desirable and good. The levels of shame and affirmation also appear to vary, based on how different family members talked about it.

Authority

Authority was not a heavily utilized way of knowing for most family members. Dad seemed to be the exception here. My mom and LaShawn mentioned that they allow themselves to be influenced by others rather than accept what they say automatically as truth. Others talked about how they relied on others' expertise for knowledge with things they could not prove themselves, such as historical events or complex mathematical concepts. Still, some family members said they relied on others' knowledge when it came to learning new skills.

Similarly, some family members talked about the way authority played more of a role when they were younger versus now. Parents and siblings were mentioned as sources of knowledge during childhood. James said he used to know about the existence of the Divine via authority, but this is no longer the case for him. He went as far as to say that he did not think that authority was a great teacher.

Reason

The importance of reason as a way of knowing varied from family member to family member. Several people agreed that it was important in some aspects of life, such as day-to-day living. For LaShawn, reason has been necessary for her survival. Others felt that reason was not a way of knowing that led to understanding deep, foundational truths. I wonder if it would be fair to say that reason is more of a basic, fundamental tool for surviving but not necessarily thriving, based on how my family responded to it as a way of knowing.

Social issues were brought up by several family members. The Israel-Palestine conflict was mentioned as something that needed to be reasoned through. Some could not reason why Palestinians could be treated so poorly, and others recognized their privilege in relation to the lives of Palestinians. Some family members mentioned their reasons for knowing that racism and sexism were actual issues that had to be managed in day-to-day life, such as in their careers. Jette said she understood that she was going to be treated differently as a woman versus being a man. She reasoned that this differential treatment could be tolerated to some extent, as long as she was well compensated.

For some, recognizing logical fallacies was important in order to decipher what was true and not true. For example, Morgan mentioned how she heard people talking about gay soldiers serving in the military and the discomfort she felt with the arguments mentioned about why they would not be fit to serve. She did not find the reasoning to be sound; someone's sexual orientation did not correlate to poor military service in a similar way that race or gender would not correlate to poor military service. Naiobi also pointed out a logical fallacy in an example I gave during our interview. She's pretty good at pointing out things that make little sense. We must protect her at all costs.

Experience

One frequently mentioned truth gleaned from experience was the responsibility for self. Several family members mentioned how they learned about finances, body autonomy, and time management through observing their habits and the habits of others. Naiobi mentioned how she has learned how to manage her time when doing schoolwork. Jette talked about how she learned to pay attention to what her body responds to energetically through trial and error. LaShawn mentioned that depending on herself versus others has given her the survival skills she now has.

Not surprisingly, how others manage interpersonal relationships has been acquired for many family members through experience. Folks talked about how they have understood their actions to impact others and vice versa. The knowledge that one can be helpful or harmful to others appeared to be understood over time. Some commented on how others have judged them and how that has shaped their ways of understanding people.

Additionally, some were not keen on leaning too much on experience. James spoke of the ways that he understands the Divine may differ empirically to the ways others understand it. In this example, he acknowledged that when it comes to the Divine, many aspects are not readily observable by everyone in the same way.

Intuition

A pattern of intuitive development seemed to be evident for several family members. They spoke of not recognizing intuition as much when they were younger and developing this way of knowing more as they got older. For some, like Nalani, intuition was not recognized as a way of knowing much, if at all. Fynn spoke of how he understood it and has experienced it somewhat but did not feel it very strongly yet as a way he understands things.

My mom, on the other hand, recognizes intuition as critical thinking. She thought intuition was important, yet something that is honed through experience. Therefore, she can intuit things about people and context. It appears to be a mostly social thing for her; she calls this reading the tea leaves.

Several family members mentioned how intuition has helped them to know about relationships with others. They commented on being able to know which people to give their energy to and which people to withhold from. Morgan mentioned how she could understand the mood of individual people and groups via her intuition. She mentioned how intuition informs how she chooses to show up in different social contexts. All of this makes sense, given how my family has been socialized to be aware of other people not to cause harm and also mitigate the effects of prejudice and bias.

Social Cognition

What folks knew through social cognition felt like the clearest example to me of different ways of knowing informing each other. Because my family has learned so much about interpersonal relationships from the other ways of knowing, it makes sense to me that there would be many intergenerational patterns of things we know through social cognition. Understanding how to find and create safety for self and others was mentioned by several family members. Some mentioned how they learned what behaviors would create closeness to or distance from others through nonverbal actions. Others talked about the depth of safety and acceptance they feel in different social situations, given their different marginalized identities.

Similarly, people talked about how they learned how to anticipate others' needs through social cognition. This came up in realms such as parenting and religion. The value of every person and the validity of others' emotions were mentioned. My dad mentioned his belief that people are sometimes unkind to others but that they can overcome this trait and essentially become kind.

Some family members talked about social cues. For some, social cues were not hard to pick up on. For others, the understanding of social cues has developed over time once they realized they were not picking up on crucial information. For Fynn, he has learned to pay more attention to body language and verbally check in if he is unsure if others are receptive to him.

Balancing Ways of Knowing

Most of my family mentioned reason as one of the ways of knowing they used the most. That being said, most people acknowledged that much of what they know is based on several ways of knowing. Some had a hard time discerning which ways of knowing they used the most, and some felt like they all blended into each other in some way or another. My dad was probably the most confident in his response that he probably leaned on authority the most.

Passing on Knowledge

When it came to passing on knowledge, there were those who could easily identify what they wanted to pass on and those who couldn't. Some family members did not initially feel like there was not much to pass on. Like with previous themes, knowledge regarding interpersonal relationships showed the strongest intergenerational link. Folks wanted to emphasize the importance of the collective when it came to investing in and caring about others. Additionally, some talked about making decisions that decrease harm for others, such as not supporting entities that contribute to harming people.

Others wanted to pass skills on to the family. Naiobi talked about sharing time management skills. Morgan talked about sharing information about metaphysical practices. Morgan also felt she indirectly shares knowledge about queer identity to others, specifically our mom and dad. James also mentioned possibly indirectly sharing things with Mom and Dad, which feels more necessary for him than sharing things with his siblings.

Flow

Flow was described in a few different ways. Some described it as being hyper-focused; others said it was almost an ultra instinct. LaShawn shared that she felt it was more about zoning in and being present as opposed to zoning out. James and Fynn described the flow state as something they don't consciously think about entering all the time.

Several folks talked about the role of focus when entering a flow state. Some mentioned that it can be hard to enter the flow state if they are distracted. This can make the entire process of finding flow take longer. Some mentioned things like cleaning or finding quiet spaces in order to enter the flow state easier. Some people naturally did these things without really thinking about them, while others had to make more of an effort to do these things.

Many family members talked about the environments in which they feel flow. Professional settings were mentioned by LaShawn and my mom as places where they could experience flow. For Mom, she felt the most flow as a nurse. For LaShawn, she experienced flow often when teaching or public speaking. They mentioned those environments feeling easy and almost automatic in how they functioned.

Activities like breathwork and yoga were mentioned as helpful for getting people into a flow state. These practices helped connect the mind and the body in a more active and present way. Morgan mentioned that this has helped her relieve tension and feel more relaxed. She said she can also think clearer when she engages in breath work meditations. A few people mentioned the importance of rest, hydration, and nutrition to being able to flow. I can definitely attest to the power of a great nap (or two) when you need the energy needed to flow.

Nature was mentioned several times as being a space where flow was found. People talked about the element of water the most. Walking on the beach or seashore, walking in water, and listening to water sounds brought flow to some people. Some mentioned their love of sand, as well. Others mentioned walking or hiking in nature more generally. For Jette, being able to walk outside without time constraints helped her flow. For my dad, camping and hiking in the wilderness put him into a flow state.

Similarly, drawing, listening to music, watching shows, and playing video games were mentioned as activities that help folks enter a flow state. These were mentioned as light ways to relax and have fun. Reading was another activity that family members talked about where they found flow. My dad and Nalani talked about how they enjoy reading books and finding flow.

Interestingly, the impact of ADHD on flow was mentioned several times. My brother mentioned how his medication has helped him focus more than he could without it. He and Morgan specifically talked about how it takes a longer time to get into the flow because of how their brains work. Nalani and Fynn mentioned having ADHD symptoms, but not an official diagnosis. Along with Naiobi, they could articulate how procrastination and distractions can impede getting tasks done.

Final Thoughts

My family has provided a rich text for us to study via their interviews. Every time I read through their responses, I learn something new and make more connections to what other family members have shared. I see the intergenerational patterns—what we have carried with us and what we have left behind. I hope you found new connections that I did not mention here, and I hope they spark new ways of understanding your own multi-identitied self.

CLOSING

There's a lot I could say in closing. Part of me also doesn't want to say anything at all. Perhaps the narrative I've outlined speaks for itself. But it doesn't feel quite complete without leaving you with something concrete to hold on to. For all the abstract and deconstructed ways I tend to look at the world, I want it to be clear where I land.

Identities matter. They impact so much of how we think and behave. There is an ideology that continues to persist by those uncomfortable with discussing the impacts of identity that "identity politics" are more divisive, more "political," and can shut down productive discourse. Phrases like "diversity, equity, and inclusion" are becoming tainted because some refuse to believe that these concepts are making a substantial difference, if they are making a difference at all. These folks tend to be white, male, middle to upper class, cisgender, able-bodied, and heterosexual. There are plenty of folks who don't fit this demographic but support the views of this demographic.

But if you ask folks who come from the margins, living at the intersections of oppressed identities, many of them will say that they do not have a chance at survival—literal and metaphorical—without increasing diversity, practicing equity, and feeling included in their personal and professional lives. They cannot distance themselves from the harmful impacts of "identity politics" in the same way people with the most privileged can. And it is irresponsible for those who have privileges where they have influence to not use it to benefit those who do not have it. Your identity impacts where you have access and influence. Use it thoughtfully and intentionally.

I don't know what the future of DEI holds. By that, I mean I don't know if the phrase "diversity, equity, and inclusion" will last a few years from now, or if it will undergo changes and a new iteration of initiatives will become palatable or trendy. DEI was very popular for mostly capitalist reasons in 2020, and the performance of caring about it has waned on many fronts. It has not waned for those whose lived experiences drastically change by taking it seriously. For us, we understand the importance of doing this work, no matter what you call it. It is work that is life-giving, that allows us to expand and exist in this world that often wants to shrink us.

So, we seek to understand, to find answers, to solve problems. We root ourselves in our wisdom learned through the physical and metaphysical. We stay knowing. And we give ourselves the space to flow and find joy in it.

How do you know things?

How do you find flow in your life?

Dig in; there's a lot to see at the root. Or in the tea leaves.

ACKNOWLEDGMENTS

So many souls came together to help bring this book to fruition.

First, a giant thank you to my family members for giving your time and permission to be interviewed and included in this project. I knew readers would resonate with your words and wisdom.

I am grateful for Sara Cannon; your *Publish and Thrive* course gave me practical tools for venturing into the world of self-publishing.

To my early readers—Tamika Flaverney, Amelia Stocking, Özlem Köse, and Ricky Bonacks—thank you for your gracious feedback that proved to make this book better.

Many thanks to my proofreader, Abiola Johnson, and your keen eye.

Thank you to my loved ones who encouraged me as I worked on getting my first book to publication.

And finally, thank you, reader, for taking a chance on this book. May you find the inspiration from it to carry on in this season of your beautiful, valuable life.

ABOUT THE AUTHOR

Niecie Jones is a multi-hyphenate professional based in Utah. She owns a psychotherapy private practice as well as a consulting company that specializes in diversity, equity, and inclusion. She co-hosts the podcast, Radical Restoration, which focuses on the well-being of millennial Black women. Niecie is always engaged in or planning her next adventure to satisfy her curiosity.

Keep up with Niecie via nieciejones.com. To support her work as a self-published and self-employed author, please leave a rating and review for this book on Amazon, Goodreads, or any other platform of your choice.

facebook.com/nieciejonesphd

instagram.com/nieciejonesphd

linkedin.com/in/nieciejonesphd